The Gospel According to Paul

A Study of the Letter to the Romans

Clifton J. Allen

BROADMAN PRESS
Nashville, Tennessee

© Copyright 1956 • Convention Press

All rights reserved

Broadman Press edition, 1973

4213–42

ISBN: 0–8054–1342–1

Dewey Decimal Classification: 227.1

Printed in the United States of America

Introduction

THE SERIOUS study of the letter to the Romans will always be a rewarding experience. It has to do with the realities and certainties of Christian salvation—with sin and forgiveness, with newness of life and moral struggle, with spiritual freedom and eternal security, with God's redemptive concern for all men. We can learn from this letter Paul's understanding of the gospel of Christ.

The purpose of this volume is to give assistance in the study of Romans itself. The author has sought to make clear the essential meaning of each passage and hence of the entire letter. Limitations of space, however, have required the omission of detailed exposition, technical explanation, illustrative matter, and inspiring application to present experience.

The readers of this volume will need to keep the text of Romans before them as they study the exposition given here. They will need also to understand that Paul's thought is often profound and at times involved. One cannot hope to grasp the message of Romans apart from diligent and purposeful study.

A word of explanation is in order. Quotations from the biblical text are usually from the King James Version. "Holy Spirit" is used instead of "Holy Ghost." In some cases the author has given his own translation. Other biblical quotations are from the American Standard Version or from the very excellent translation of the New Testament by Charles B. Williams.

The author wishes to express his appreciation to Drs. J. N. Barnette and A. V. Washburn, of the Sunday School Department of the Baptist Sunday School Board, for the invitation to prepare this textbook for the Sunday School Training Course and, first of all, for a week of special Bible study in the churches. It is his earnest prayer that this small volume may guide many persons to a fuller comprehension of the letter to the Romans and to a firmer faith in the truth of the saving gospel.

Also, the author acknowledges with grateful appreciation the permission of the publishers of the works cited to use brief quotations from their respective publications. References to these works will be found at the close of the chapters.

CLIFTON J. ALLEN

Contents

1. Paul's Introduction to Romans   1
2. Man's Plight in Sin   20
3. The Divine Remedy   39
4. Saved by Grace   52
5. Christian Sanctification   65
6. Life in the Spirit   80
7. God's Purpose in History   95
8. Righteousness in Christian Living   110
9. Ambassador for Christ   127

1

Paul's Introduction to Romans

Romans 1:1-17

THE LETTER to the Romans is one of the most important things ever written. It takes its place alongside the Gospel of John and the letter to the Ephesians on the highest level of revealed truth. No one who undertakes seriously to understand the Christian gospel can pass it by. Though but a relatively brief letter, it is the most significant work ever produced in the field of Christian theology.

This letter deals directly with the basic issues in human experience: How can man come into right relationship with God? How can he achieve inner peace and experience moral victory? What is there to give meaning to life in the midst of suffering and to give certainty to faith in a world of evil? What is man's duty to his fellow man? What is his responsibility for the life of the world? In the letter to the Romans we have the divine answer to these questions.

This letter is not a dull treatise on theological abstractions. It is a classic in theology and a masterpiece that pulsates with life. It is warm with the lifeblood of redemptive truth. It is the testimony of a daring spiritual explorer. It rings with the certainty of experience. For those who are teachable, the letter to the Romans is persuasive and convincing. For the spiritually sensitive, it indicts the conscience and inspires action. For the perplexed and despairing, it speaks certainty and consolation.

At the heart of this letter is the throbbing spirit of world missions. It is missionary throughout. There is good news for all men. The gospel of Christ is the power of God for salvation to everyone who believes. "There is no difference between the Jew and the Greek: for the same Lord over all is rich unto all that call upon him. For whosoever shall call upon the name of the Lord shall be saved" (10:12–13). Indeed, the letter closes with the writer's vision of the gospel being preached to all men, that the nations might come to the obedience of faith (16:26).

I. Paul the Apostle

We can never understand the letter to the Romans apart from an understanding of the writer himself. As a preparation for the study of the letter, let us look, first of all, at the writer.

Paul was a Jew, of the tribe of Benjamin. He testified, "that after the most straitest sect of our religion I lived a Pharisee" (Acts 26:5). Though born in Tarsus in Cilicia—and born a Roman citizen as well—he had been brought up at the feet of Gamaliel, one of the foremost teachers of Judaism. With loyalty to his ancestral faith and zeal for the Mosaic law, he advanced beyond those of his own age and in early manhood became the recognized leader of the first general persecution of Christians. In humble confession of his misguided zeal, he declared late in life, " I persecuted this way unto the death, binding and delivering into prisons both men and women" (Acts 22:4).

But something happened to the bloodthirsty persecutor. On the Damascus road, he met Jesus Christ. Paul saw himself the chief of sinners, though blameless in observing the externals of the Mosaic law. He discovered that his own righteousness by the law had not broken the power of pride and selfishness in his heart. When he met Jesus of Nazareth, alive from the dead, Paul realized his own moral impotence and spiritual rebellion. More important still, he saw in Jesus the expression of God's love for sinful men and the fulfilment of God's promise of the Messiah. And there, on the Damascus road, the archenemy of Christianity bowed his will to the Lord Jesus Christ. He was justified by faith. He experienced the grace of God.

But something else wonderful happened to Paul on the

Damascus road. He began to hear with perfect clarity the words of the risen Lord: "I have appeared unto thee for this purpose, to make thee a minister and a witness both of these things which thou hast seen, and of those things in the which I will appear unto thee; delivering thee from the people, and from the Gentiles, unto whom now I send thee, to open their eyes, and to turn them from darkness to light, and from the power of Satan unto God, that they may receive forgiveness of sins, and inheritance among them which are sanctified by faith" (Acts 26:16–18).

Paul was not disobedient to that heavenly vision. In preparation for that mission he withdrew into Arabia, there to spend three years in a tryst with God. Paul needed to think through his new experience in Christ. He needed to rethink his understandings of the Old Testament revelation. He needed to get, not from men, not even the apostles, but from heaven itself, a revelation of the deeper meaning of the gospel and an understanding of God's plan of the ages: "that the Gentiles should be fellowheirs, and of the same body, and partakers of his promise in Christ by the gospel" (Eph. 3:6). In the school of prayer alone could he learn that "there is no difference between the Jew and the Greek: for the same Lord over all is rich unto all that call upon him" (10:12).

When Paul returned from Arabia he knew the will of God for his life. In a very real sense the gospel had been revealed to him. He had a message to preach. He could say, "my gospel."

The time had not come for Paul to embark directly on the fulfilment of his mission. He had to learn lessons through persecution and waiting. But when the call of the Holy Spirit came to the church in Antioch, Paul was ready to launch out on a world mission with a world gospel. He made three missionary journeys into Asia Minor and Greece, dependent almost altogether upon his own manual labor for support, preaching the gospel in the cities of major importance, and founding churches through which the work of evangelization and teaching could go on.

By tireless preaching and teaching, and a series of letters written to some of the churches, the heroic apostle pushed the Christian movement forward. In cities like Ephesus and Corinth, as well as in many other places, he learned that the straightforward proclamation of the truth about Christ is the power of God unto salvation. He saw life on every moral, intellectual, and social level changed by the message of the cross and the resurrection. He saw the masses of people, victims of false philosophy and vain deceit, of idolatry and superstition, of lust and greed; and his heart reached out toward them with a feeling of deepest spiritual concern. With inexpressible compassion for his own people, he longed for their salvation. With an imperial view of the gospel, Paul yearned to proclaim it in Rome and to the farthest limits of the Empire in Spain.

Paul was, first and foremost, a missionary. The chief aspect of his witness was the proclamation of the gospel, with emphasis on the doctrines of salvation: the way men become right with God, the life worthy of those who acknowledge Christ as Saviour, and the sovereign purpose of God which gives assurance that the saving work of Christ will come to fruition in the redemption of men.

This is the man who wrote the letter to the Romans. This letter bore a witness from experience. It came from his soul and from the laboratory of life, from a person to whom had come by revelation the very oracles of God in Christ.

II. Occasion for the Letter

Before we come to deal with the contents of the letter directly, it is needful to consider the occasion for its being written. We need an over-all perspective as a background for our study. There are important facts which constitute a frame of reference for interpretation.

1. Authorship and Date

The author of the letter declares that he is Paul the apostle. As already indicated, we accept this without reservation. The evidence for Pauline authorship is overwhelmingly conclusive. The style and vocabulary are Paul's. The theme is the central emphasis of Paul's preaching and teaching. The letter deals with issues that were the burden of Paul's ministry. The doctrinal content of the letter is the natural expression of Paul's background, experience, and mission. Romans is obviously the product of the same mind and heart as Galatians, and the two letters to the Corinthians—letters almost universally acknowledged to have come from Paul's pen. Paul's authorship is so well established that it is a "closed question."[1]

The letter was written from Corinth in the spring of A.D. 57 or 58. Putting together what we know of Paul's activities from the facts given by Luke in Acts 20–21 and what Paul himself says in Romans 15:22–29, we can rather definitely reconstruct the situation in which the letter was written.

After a prolonged stay in Ephesus, Paul had gone into Greece, to Corinth, where he remained three months. Conditions in the Corinthian church were much improved. He had been collecting an offering from the Gentile churches, especially those in Macedonia and Greece, for the poverty-stricken saints in Jerusalem. Paul was anxious to take the offering to Jerusalem as an expression of good will on the part of the Gentile Christians. He was determined to do his utmost, even to the point of risking his life, to effect unity between the Jewish and Gentile parties within the Christian movement. His purpose was to proceed from Jerusalem to Spain by way of Rome. But now he felt that his work was largely completed in Asia and Greece (15: 23), so that he could turn his attention to a long-cherished dream to preach in Rome and beyond. While he waited, he had a relaxed opportunity for writing.

2. Missionary Objective

But the question arises, What was the real occasion for this letter? What was Paul's specific purpose in writing it? On this point there is considerable difference of opinion. E. F. Scott argues that Paul's chief purpose was "to prepare the way for his coming visit" as a means of enlisting the assistance of the Roman church in carrying forward his mission to Spain and other remote areas.[2] He insists that Paul was concerned to introduce himself to the church in such a way as to remove the grave suspicion about him which had been spread abroad by the Jewish party in Jerusalem. This, according to Scott, would be a means of insuring co-operation from the Roman church in carrying out his missionary objective.

With this view C. H. Dodd is in essential agreement, for he says: "It was not any internal conditions in the church at Rome that called forth the letter, but the development of Paul's own plans. . . . It was important for him to secure the sympathy of the church of Rome. He therefore sets before them a comprehensive and reasoned statement of the fundamentals of Christianity as he understood it, which is at the same time an *apologia* for the principles and methods of his Gentile mission."[3] In the light of Paul's letter, the Christians in Rome would decide whether he was worthy of their support.

3. Doctrinal Objective

Anders Nygren concurs that the immediate occasion for Paul's writing was "to prepare the congregation at Rome for his coming,"[4] but he warns against drawing a false conclusion as to the apostle's larger purpose. Nygren insists that "Paul is dealing with problems on which life hangs both for him and for the congregation to which he writes."[5] We are further reminded that the epistle, while taking on the form of a letter, was doctrinal writing to the core and was essentially a theological treatise.

We still face the problem: Was the purpose of the letter to the Romans chiefly to cultivate support for a great missionary objective, or was it chiefly to present a comprehensive and logical exposition of the centralities of the gospel? It was both. But it was more the latter than the first. Paul had a consuming passion to make known the truth about salvation. He wanted to set forth the full content of that great doctrine: the need for salvation, the way of salvation, and the fruits of salvation. He therefore dedicated the utmost powers of his mind and heart to the production of this letter. He brought to the task the content of divine revelation, the insights of his own experience, and the burden of his concern that the message of salvation should be proclaimed to all men everywhere.

III. SALUTATION—1:1-7

In New Testament times it was customary for a letter to begin with a salutation identifying the writer, addressing the persons to whom the letter was sent, and giving a brief word of greeting. Therefore, Paul began his letter like that. A similar example is seen in the letter of the Jerusalem church to the Gentile churches (Acts 15:23). Paul uniformly began his letters in this fashion.

1. *The Writer and His Message* (*vv. 1-5*)

The opening verses of Romans, however, are distinctive. Paul does more than sign his name; he introduces himself in keeping with the fact that he was largely unknown to the Christians in Rome. He says enough about himself to prepare his readers for the content of his letter. Again, in brief but weighty words, Paul sums up the essence of what he is about to write. And finally, he adds words describing the character of those to whom he is writing and connects them with himself in a bond of fellowship. They, too, are "the called of Jesus Christ."

In these five verses Paul tells us six things about himself.

(1) He delighted to call himself "a servant of Jesus Christ." What higher distinction could he want? This really means bondslave. It had a wealth of meaning for the apostle. It carried the idea of commitment to the will of Christ. He was in no sense his own, for he had been bought with a price. The Lord's absolute ownership is an important concept for a Christian. The full force of this word is found in its object—Jesus Christ. And this also emphasizes the fact that Paul's life, as well as his theology, was Christocentric.

(2) Next, Paul states that he was "called to be an apostle." Though not one of the twelve, he was in no sense inferior to them. Paul had no occasion here to emphasize the authority of his apostleship in the way that he did in writing to the Galatians and the Corinthians. Even so, the fact that he had been divinely called to the unique ministry of an apostle gave force and meaning to what he would write.

(3) Again, he recorded his deep conviction that he was "separated," or set apart, to the gospel of God. He acknowledged God's purpose in his life. He felt a sense of commitment. He would let nothing come between him and his mission to preach the gospel. Already before this he had written to the Galatians to affirm his conviction that God had separated him from his mother's womb and called him by his grace to reveal his Son in him that he might preach among the Gentiles (Gal. 1:15–16). Paul believed in a divine call. He was eager for the Romans to think of him, not as one grasping for an office or claiming authority in himself, but as one under appointment from God, ordained under the will of the Lord and sent forth with a heavenly mission.

(4) After setting forth in briefest fashion what the gospel of God is, Paul went on to declare that through Christ he had "received grace and apostleship, for obedience to the faith among all nations, for his name." Paul could not forget the pride and rebellion of his unregenerated life and the exceeding greatness of his sin before he met Jesus on the Damascus road. Nothing but God's grace could have conquered Paul's pride and subdued his stubborn heart. Hence, he delighted to acknowledge his indebtedness to grace for his redemption and also for the unmerited privilege of preaching the gospel.

(5) His apostleship, also, was a gift of grace. He had not merited so great honor. God had chosen him, not because of his merit, but to demonstrate through him the effectual working of his own power (Eph. 3:7). There was a divine purpose, as Paul says in verse 5: "for obedience to the faith." Paul likely means "for obedience inspired by

faith," or "the obedience which springs from faith." [6] This is a fundamental concept in Paul's gospel: obedience springs from within; faith is the spring of action.

(6) Paul's final word about himself is that the compelling motive for all that he had done and all that he purposed to do was "for his name." Throughout the years of his saved life he had been constrained constantly by the love of Christ, so that his supreme concern was to honor the Name above every name.

Now let us look at the heart of this salutation and note what Paul has to say in his epitome of the gospel. First of all, it is the gospel of God. It is from God and about God and for God. To us the word "gospel" has become almost trite. But to Paul it meant "good news" indeed. The gospel in which his hope rested, which he was so eager to preach in Rome and elsewhere, had a divine origin, therefore divine authority. It had been announced by the prophets in the Old Testament Scriptures. It was the fulfilment of a promise made by God to the children of Israel. Paul thus registered his faith in and fidelity to the Holy Scriptures, though he had been falsely represented as undermining and distorting the Mosaic law and the teaching of the Old Testament.

The central truth about the gospel is that it concerns God's Son, "Jesus Christ our Lord." The gospel revelation came through Christ. His life and death and resurrection are the chief facts of the gospel. The apostle went on to say that Jesus was both human and divine. He was "of the seed of David according to the flesh," but he was "declared to be the Son of God ... by the resurrection from the dead." As the Son of David, Jesus was of the royal line: he was the King promised to the Jews. The emphasis in verse 3 is upon the fact of his genuine humanity. He was in fact the Son of man.

A more wonderful truth had to be added, namely, that the same Jesus is the very Son of God. There are varying interpretations about the meaning of these words. Moffatt translates them, "installed as Son of God with power by the

Spirit of holiness when he was raised from the dead." Probably the true meaning is found in Williams' translation: "Who on the physical side became a descendant of David, and on the holy spiritual side proved to be God's Son in power by the resurrection from the dead." It was not the resurrection which made him God's Son, but it confirmed every claim that he had made about himself. This was "the miracle of miracles."

"The spirit of holiness" is equated by some with "Holy Spirit." Others hold that it refers to Jesus in his essential nature, which was marked by perfect holiness. Let it be noted that "the resurrection from the dead" should be translated "the resurrection of the dead." Christ was the first fruits of the resurrection. His resurrection suggests by implication the general resurrection of the dead which is assured by his victory over death.

Let us then sum up the truth Paul presented. He declares that he had a calling from God, and, because of that, he is set apart for the gospel. It has to do with Jesus Christ our Lord, through whom God revealed himself to men, through whom the reign of death has been conquered, a gospel which finds its meaning and power in the risen Lord.

2. *The Church in Rome* (*vv. 6-7*)

The closing part of Paul's salutation indicates the ones to whom his letter was written. Before considering the content of this salutation in detail, it will be helpful to observe some general matters about the church in Rome.

Let us note that this church was not founded by the apostle Paul. When he wrote this letter, the church was already in existence, and Paul had never been to Rome. Furthermore, the church in Rome was so well established that Paul could give thanks to God "that your faith is spoken of throughout the whole world" (1:8). Evidently the Christians in the capital of the Empire had given a witness that had proved a source of inspiration to believers in many places.

How the church in Rome came to be organized and by whom cannot be definitely known. There were persons from Rome in Jerusalem on Pentecost. It is most likely that some of the converts of the earliest apostolic preaching in Jerusalem returned to Rome and became the nucleus of the church there. Travel was common, especially to and from Rome. It would have been most natural, also, for some persons from Rome, who chanced to be in Antioch or Ephesus or Philippi or Corinth during one of the periods of Paul's ministry, to have heard him preach and have received the gospel. They would have returned to Rome and joined themselves with the saints there. This would explain, in part, the long list of Paul's acquaintances in chapter 16.

The church was made up of both Jews and Gentiles, though the group was obviously more largely composed of Gentiles. We may safely assume that among the saints in Rome there were people of all classes, including some who were influential but likely a much larger number of middle-class and lower than middle-class folk. Paul felt that they needed his ministry, for he long planned to go to Rome and longed to share with them some spiritual gift that would contribute to their stability and fruitfulness; while at the same time he expected to receive from them encouragement and stimulation. Surely, the church at Rome had not made much dent on the militarism and paganism of the capital, but doubtless it had become a spiritual fellowship that had in it the potential influence of redemptive power.

There is absolutely no convincing evidence that Peter was responsible for founding the church in Rome, regardless of the insistent claims of Catholicism to that effect. The claims that he was ever in Rome are based on tradition rather than established fact. If he was there—and it is altogether possible that he was—it would have been a considerable time after the church was founded. All the evidences we have point to his being there, if he was, even later than the time of the writing of Paul's letter.

One other general comment may be made about the church at Rome. When Paul wrote his letter to the Philippians, while he was actually in Rome, which was several years after the writing of this letter, there were elements in the Roman church bitterly antagonistic to the apostle (Phil. 1:15–18). When his first defense finally came, or first trial, none of the Roman Christians stood by him—all his friends had forsaken him. We ought, therefore, to realize that the church in Rome had to give its witness against an imperialism that declared Caesar to be Lord and did its utmost to destroy every rival faith.

Now let us turn to the very meaningful words with which Paul's salutation closes. The believers in Rome were "the called of Jesus Christ." They acknowledged that they were "called to be Christ's," that is, they acknowledged Christ as Lord and felt that they belonged to him. More than that, they were "beloved of God." In a special way they had found favor with God and had received the blessings of his grace. The particular force, however, of this phrase is to point out the persons to whom the letter was sent—not all the people in Rome, but the ones who stood in a special relationship to God because of their faith in Christ.

Greater emphasis still should be given to the fact that these Christians were called saints. They were "holy ones." This is exactly what Christians are, all of them. A saint, in New Testament meaning, is not a person who has died, or even a living person of rare piety, but a believer in Christ, justified by faith, and set apart for the purposes of God by virtue of his being a child of God.

The members of our churches today have urgent need to realize that they are saints in fact, so that they ought to recognize the obligation resting upon them to become saintly in conduct. Holiness is not just an ideal for Christians; it is an obligation because of what the Christian is as a temple of the Holy Spirit.

The apostle then adds his greeting: "Grace to you and peace from God our Father, and the Lord Jesus Christ."

This is the expression of the apostle's wish for his readers, or a prayer in their behalf, that they might experience the unmerited goodness of God and the peace which come through his forgiveness and the activity of his Spirit. These are the Heavenly Father's gifts imparted to men in and through the Lord Jesus Christ.

Interestingly enough, in this brief salutation Paul four times uses the term "Jesus Christ," and twice adds the title "Lord." This was not a mere repetition of words. It declared something of the supremacy of Christ in Paul's own life and in his concept of the gospel. For him, Jesus of Nazareth was the Messiah of Israel, the living Lord.

Here, then, we have a church. It is well established in the Imperial City. The Christians who constitute its fellowship have a world mission. Paul yearns to share with them his understanding of the gospel and his vision of its objective.

IV. PERSONAL GREETING—1:8–15

Paul had never been to Rome, but he had for a long time wanted to go. Even so, he felt a strong bond of friendship with many of the Christians there, as the personal greetings in 16:3–15 so clearly show. Far more important, however, his interest in Rome was associated with his sense of the stewardship of the gospel. This needs to be kept in mind as we explore the rich store of truth in these verses of intimate personal greeting following the more formal salutation with which the letter begins.

In the personal greeting we learn much that provides a background of understanding for the remaining part of the letter. Paul wants the Roman Christians to understand his feeling toward them and his conviction about the gospel. He therefore writes in an intimate vein about the deep aspirations of his heart.

1. Prayer of Thanksgiving and Concern (vv. 8–10)

The greeting begins with a prayer of thanksgiving. One cause for special thanksgiving is the faith of the Roman

Christians. Paul rejoices in the fact that they are believers in Christ and, more particularly, that their faith is widely known. He must have in mind the situation of the Roman Christians. They are in the capital city, the seat of imperial power, in which mighty combines of evil seek to destroy spiritual religion and fight against all the ideals of the Christian faith. The worship of the emperor, the idolatry of pagan religions, the excesses of brutality and lust, the vulgarity and pride and atheism of the well-to-do, and the deadening effects of militarism and secularism, all constitute mighty opposition to the survival of the Christian group. But their faith is "spoken of throughout the whole world." Paul feels the deepest concern for his fellow Christians and offers unceasing prayer for them. He knows the strategic mission and the grave perils of a church at the very center of the Empire.

A second aspect of Paul's unceasing prayer relates to his own desire to go to Rome. For a long time this had been a dream. Now he prays with intense earnestness that God will prosper his plans to visit the church in Rome. His only hope for achieving his purpose will of course depend upon the blessing of God. Now as always he recognizes that his life must be at the center of the will of God, and he hopes that it will be a part of the divine plan to prosper his own plans with respect to going to Rome. But first, he must go to Jerusalem to take the offering of the Gentile churches to the poor saints in Judea. Paul knows only too well that his mission is fraught with great hazard. And so he prays— and later on he will beseech the Christians in Rome to join him in prayer for the same objective (15:30–32)—that he may carry out his plans.

2. *Desire to Visit Rome* (*vv. 11–15*)

Paul's desire to go to Rome is in no sense selfish. Note what he says: "That I may impart unto you some spiritual gift, to the end ye may be established." Paul wanted to share his understanding of the gospel, his faith in Christ, and his testimony as to the mighty power of the gospel in saving men, both Jews and Gentiles. Paul thinks, not without justification, that he can make a contribution to the strength and stability and effective witness of the church in Rome.

And along with this, with sincere humility Paul expresses his assurance that he will himself receive a blessing from going to Rome. He needs the encouragement of their faith, just as they need the spiritual gifts God has entrusted to him. Thus there can be mutual reinforcement and blessing. No Christian shares instruction and faith and encouragement with others without receiving in return much to increase his capacity and joy, without receiving much that contributes to his own strength and growth.

To emphasize this point Paul declares again, "Oftentimes I purposed to come unto you." Rome had been a sort of goal, but always something had happened to obstruct the fulfilment of his plan. Such is the meaning of what seems to us an awkward expression, "was let hitherto." The burdens of his work in Greece and Macedonia and Asia Minor had held him there. He hopes now that soon he can accomplish his purpose to go to Rome that he may get fruits for the gospel there, just as he has done among the Gentiles in such cities as Corinth and Ephesus.

Paul had an overwhelming sense of obligation to all men. He felt himself to be a debtor "both to the wise, and to the unwise." He thus thought of all classes of people, the highly cultured and the grossly illiterate, the well-to-do and the underprivileged, persons of high standing and those without standing, the wise and the foolish. Paul was a true universalist in his view of humanity. He believed in the worth of every individual, and he believed that the gospel of Christ was meant for all men.

At the center of Paul's being there was a passion to preach the gospel. He was ready and willing to preach the gospel in Rome. He was conscious of a stewardship of truth. He knew the need of the Christians in Rome for indoctrination and encouragement. He knew the need of the non-Christians for the message of salvation through

Christ. Therefore, he longed to share the good news of redemption and righteousness. The purpose of Paul's greeting was to establish a sort of rapport with the Christians in Rome. This would serve to prepare their minds and hearts for the contents of his letter and for his ministry in their midst which he hoped soon to realize.

V. THEME OF THE LETTER—1:16–17

In these two verses Paul states the central theme of his letter. He wanted to give a full exposition of the gospel message. With a great burden of responsibility, he wanted to silence forever the false teaching of salvation by works and to establish beyond all refutation the truth that salvation rests upon the righteousness of God upon the one condition of faith in Jesus Christ.

1. *The Gospel the Power of God unto Salvation (v. 16)*

Paul knew that in the minds of many the gospel seemed to be foolishness. In Athens the philosophers listened with curiosity until he spoke of the resurrection of the dead; then they began to mock. In city after city his preaching had met the strongest opposition. To the worldly wise it seemed foolishness. With the wicked it stirred up bitter resentment. In the empire of the Caesars it told about another Lord. Nevertheless, Paul stated his position almost at the beginning of his letter: "I am not ashamed of the gospel of Christ." Already he had written to the Galatians, "I bear in my body the marks of the Lord Jesus" (6:17). He was anxious to go to Rome to preach this same Christ and to proclaim his gospel.

This gospel is "the power of God unto salvation to every one that believeth." The word translated "power" is *dunamis*, from which we get our word dynamite. There is spiritual dynamic in the message of Christ. It is not just an idea or a philosophic system. It has in it the very power of God. In the gospel there is the power of divine love, the power of eternal truth, the power of moral judgment, and the power of the living Spirit. Paul had known this power in his own experience, first, when he met Jesus on the Damascus road and, second, as the bondslave of Christ and ambassador of the Lord.

The gospel had demonstrated its power wherever Paul had preached it. It had brought salvation to everyone that believed. In Antioch and Philippi and Corinth and Ephesus and even Athens, the gospel had won converts. They were multiplying by the thousands. Men were being lifted from the depths of moral ruin and brought down from the heights of intellectual pride to find in Jesus Christ freedom from sin and peace with God. So it was for every one who believed, "to the Jew first, and also to the Greek." It came to the Jew first, but it was meant also for the Greek; that is, it was meant for all men. Paul was not afraid to risk the same gospel in the city of Rome. He knew that it would prove there as everywhere a redeeming power in the hearts of men. There is no other power like the power of the gospel. It changes the very inner nature of those who believe in it. It effects spiritual renewal and moral reconstruction in one's total personality. It is this power of the gospel which is the hope of a sin-cursed world.

2. The Gospel the Revelation of the Righteousness of God (v. 17)

Paul went on to say, "Therein is the righteousness of God revealed from faith to faith: as it is written, The just shall live by faith." This is Paul's theme. We need to get fixed clearly in mind what he means by "the righteousness of God." Nygren says that "the righteousness of God is a righteousness originating in God, prepared by God, revealed in the gospel and therein offered to us." [7] John Knox says that the term as Paul uses it "designates not so much God's own righteousness as an act of God on behalf of men." [8] That is, it is a justifying or reconciling act on the part of God, which gives us a new status before him. Dodd thinks that the central idea in righteousness is the vindication of right.[9] Right is vindicated in the deliverance of man from the power of evil.

In reality, the righteousness of God includes these ideas and more. It denotes a God-kind of righteousness. It is intrinsic to the nature of God, inherent in the being of God, but it is offered to men by faith in Jesus Christ. On this basis God imputes his own righteousness to the believer. Thus a person, though he is sinful, is given right standing with God—thus he becomes a Christian. This is justification. But the righteousness of God goes beyond that: it includes also sanctification.[10] Salvation means righteousness imputed to us and righteousness achieved by us. The righteousness of God is first of all received by faith, an undeserved gift; but then it becomes operative in the new life through union with Christ. The righteousness bestowed on the Christian is meant to produce righteousness in the Christian. And the righteousness in the Christian is meant to be demonstrated in a life of upright conduct and kingdom service.

Emphasis is put on the fact, right at the beginning, that the righteousness of God must be received by faith. It is "from faith unto faith." It is all of faith and nothing more. It begins with faith and leads on to deeper faith. Nothing else can avail to obtain a right standing with God—neither culture, nor race, nor inheritance, nor works. Indeed it is true: "The just shall live by faith."

The apostle is going to deal with this great theme in his letter: the need of sinful men for the righteousness of God (1:18 to 3:20), the way of righteousness through justification (3:21 to 4:25), the provision of righteousness through grace (5:1–21), and the new life of righteousness through the Spirit (6:1 to 8:39). After dealing with the purpose of God in history (9:1 to 11:36), Paul will portray righteousness demonstrated in everyday living (12:1 to 15:13). He will close his letter with the challenge of Christian missions whereby the message of righteousness is to be preached to the whole world (15:14 to 16:27).

Paul yearned to make known the whole sweep of gospel truth. He understood the issues of his day, the reality of sin and redemption, and the timeless character of the gospel message. What is more natural than that he would seek to set forth in his letter to the Christians in Rome his magnum opus of the saving gospel? Such a purpose seems implied in the apostle's statement of his theme, and it seems to be confirmed by the weighty exposition of Christian doctrine which makes up the content of his letter.

---

[1] C. H. Dodd, *The Epistle of Paul to the Romans* (New York: Harper and Brothers, n. d.), p. xiii

[2] E. F. Scott, *Paul's Epistle to the Romans* (London: Student Christian Movement Press, 1947), pp. 18–27

[3] Dodd, *op. cit.*, p. xxv

[4] Anders Nygren, *Commentary on Romans*, Translation by Carl C. Rasmussen (Philadelphia: Muhlenberg Press, 1949), p. 5

[5] *Ibid.*, p. 7

[6] A. T. Robertson, *Word Pictures in the New Testament*, Vol. IV (Nashville: The Sunday School Board of the Southern Baptist Convention), p. 324

[7] Nygren, *op. cit.*, p. 76

[8] John Knox, *The Interpreter's Bible,* Vol. 9 (New York: Abingdon Press, 1954), p. 393

[9] Dodd, *op. cit.*, p. 13

[10] Robertson, *op. cit.*, p. 327

2

Man's Plight in Sin

Romans 1:18 to 3:20

PAUL was a realist. He knew the fearful reality of sin, and so he dealt with it in keeping with its seriousness. What he wrote to the Romans—and wrote in his other letters as well—cuts straight across the fancies and theories of much modern thought. His portrayal of evil in natural man shows how utterly erroneous is the claim of the humanist that man is inherently good; it shows how absolutely false is the claim of the moralist that man through a process of education can be trained to be good. Paul understood man's real dilemma: his moral nature is corrupted by evil. There is something radically wrong at the center of his being. The unredeemed man is in bondage to the law of sin and death.

Therefore, Paul began his exposition of the gospel at the point of man's most basic need. Man needs salvation because he stands condemned in the sight of God. In the logical mind of Paul, there seemed no other way to begin.

According to C. H. Dodd, "Paul should not be understood as propounding a rigid theory of the total depravity of human nature."[1] But that is exactly what Paul did do—provided we observe what is meant by "total depravity." The apostle did not mean that man is totally depraved to the extent that he is incapable of some good. In response to the promptings of conscience, the natural man may do good deeds. But this does not deny the fact that his whole nature has been affected by evil. Total depravity means that the core of man's being is selfish, that he is morally impotent because his will is enslaved, and that he is utterly helpless to achieve salvation in and through himself. This fact Paul propounds with as much rigidity as language can affirm and with inexorable logic.

In this first section of his letter, 1:18 to 3:20, Paul sets forth man's universal guilt and his need for something he cannot do for himself. Both Jews and Gentiles (Paul used these terms to encompass the whole of humanity) are condemned: "they are all under sin" (3:9). The plight of man is his sinfulness. If he is ever to be saved, it must be by the grace of God and the power of God. Let us consider then the universal condemnation of man in sin.

I. The Wrath of God—1:18

For some the idea of the wrath of God is untenable. We do need to be careful lest we misunderstand what is meant by this phrase. Divine wrath is a fact. There is no use to deny it. But this does not argue against another fact, namely, that God is perfect love. It is the reality of divine love which makes all the more terrible the reality of divine wrath.

The wrath of God is the necessary reaction of his holiness to evil. He takes issue with sin. Because of his moral nature, his whole being reacts against immorality. If there were no capacity for wrath on the part of God, his holiness would be without moral quality and strength. But again let us keep our thinking straight. The wrath of God never means that God becomes mad with rage. He never acts with uncontrolled anger. He never burns with a desire to get revenge. God hates sin, but he loves the sinner.

Now Paul says that "the wrath of God is revealed from heaven against all ungodliness and unrighteousness of men." The expression "is revealed" is exactly the same as in verse 17. The wrath of God is a necessary counterpart of the righteousness of God. The righteousness of God is revealed in the gospel of salvation. The wrath of God is revealed directly from heaven in judgment on wickedness. This does not point to the final judgment. The wrath of God will, of course, be revealed at the end of the world.

But Paul says it "is being continuously revealed" now. The righteous wrath of God against wickedness is in evidence everywhere, if people are only willing to see.

This revelation of wrath is against "all ungodliness and unrighteousness of men." Nothing gets by. And there is no evil—not even one vulgar word or one so-called white lie—which escapes the wrath of God. "Ungodliness" has special reference to impiety or irreligion and "unrighteousness" to immorality. It covers "all transgressions of both tables of the law."[2] These two words must not be thought of as markedly different. To be ungodly is to be unrighteous. Irreligion leads always to immorality.

In a sense, verse 18 is introductory to this whole section. God's wrath is against every kind of sin on the part of all men. The whole human race is involved. And all men are alike in that they "hold the truth in unrighteousness." They try to "hold down the truth." They resent the indictments of conscience and try to suppress the truth which makes them aware of their moral accountability before God. They fight against the truth that reveals their guilt and condemns them as lost and undone. Men deny the fact of moral guilt. They pretend to believe that there is no hell. They try to laugh off the fact that this is a moral universe and that man will reap as he sows. They rationalize and speculate, all because they do not want to face the truth that God's wrath against sin is real.

II. Pride and Idolatry—1:19-23

It seems fairly certain that the remaining part of chapter 1 refers primarily to the Gentiles. What Paul said applies also to the Jews, but he had chiefly in mind the pagan world and the people who did not have the law of God.

1. *Light Rejected* (*vv. 19-20*)

The Gentiles had not had the law, but they had not been without a revelation. God had revealed himself to them through his created universe. They had had light. If only they had been willing to follow it! We are not to conclude that the Gentiles had no need of the gospel or that they had all the light they needed. What Paul means is that they had had enough light to be morally responsible.

God had manifested himself to men. "That which may be known of God" does not mean all that is knowable but rather, "what can be known of God is clear to their inner moral sense" (Williams). All around the pagan there is evidence of God. The created universe speaks convincingly about its Maker. God the invisible becomes visible in his handiwork. All that he made speaks of "his everlasting power" (ASV). The word for "Godhead" does not mean divine Personality but divine Nature, the attributes of which are power, goodness, justice, mercy, and eternity. One cannot look out on the world with open mind without seeing the evidence of both omnipotence and omniscience.

Therefore, the Gentiles were without excuse. They could not blame God. Pagans everywhere stand condemned not because of God's arbitrariness and not because God has any delight in their condemnation. They are condemned, because they have shut their eyes to the light that would have pointed them to God. They have rejected the truth that would have given them direction.

2. *God Desecrated* (*vv. 21–23*)

Paul goes on to explain the very heart of such impiety or ungodliness. Though faced with the fact of God, they refuse to give him glory or to treat him as God. They neither show reverence nor give thanks. They push God away with indifference because they are not willing to yield themselves to him. God has sought to reveal himself to men. But the natural man tries to hold down the truth. On this basis the judgment of God is surely justified.

With respect to the Gentiles, Paul says that they "became vain in their imaginations, and their foolish heart was darkened." Nothing is so empty as vanity. The sure way to be left in darkness is unwillingness to learn.

Always man makes a fool of himself when he tries to devise a substitute for God. This may take any one of a hundred forms. He tries to drag the incorruptible God down to his own corruptible level because he wants his own corruptible living to be approved. Or he makes a god out of birds or beasts or creeping things because he wants a god he can control. The natural man makes a god out of something material because he is not willing to make the material elements in his life secondary to the spiritual.

Thus we can see that man does not really become irreligious. He simply creates a religion to suit himself. He worships at the altar of selfishness or lust or fear or force or magic or beauty. But all such religion is vain. It leaves man in his own sinful state. He is without adequate moral incentive, without spiritual strength, without deliverance from evil, without a key to the meaning of existence, and without justification and forgiveness before the holy God.

The pagan world through the centuries has confirmed these words of Paul. The most absurd and shameful idolatry has resulted from indifference to the true God. "Even to-day the blindest infidelity is coincident with the most insufferable conceit."[3] Ungodliness is the certain fruitage of the mind and heart without God.

III. The Depths of Moral Ruin—1:24–32

The accompaniment and the result of irreligion is immorality. Ungodliness and unrighteousness go together. But the basic explanation of man's moral ruin is false religion. "A wrong relation to God is the ultimate cause of man's corruption."[4]

In verses 24–32 we have the most realistic description in the Bible of the depths to which evil plunges men. Paul uses chaste words, but he paints a picture of indescribable wickedness and corruption. Paul had seen enough of life in Corinth and Ephesus, as well as many other places, to understand how far sin will go. What he wrote was not a morbid view of life but a declaration of truth from God that men may see their ruin and repent.

In verses 24, 26, and 28 we have a thrice-repeated declaration of the judgment of divine wrath: "God gave them up"—the same word in each instance. These three declarations of judgment may not indicate progressive stages of intensification of divine punishment but rather different aspects of punishment.[5] There is, however, a direct causal connection between what man does and what God does. The connective in each of these three verses points back to verses 19–23. When men turn away from God and substitute man-made gods for the true God, he deals with them in keeping with the demands of his own moral nature. Punitive justice has to operate. When men cast God off, his wrath against ungodliness is revealed in judgment. As Robertson remarks, "These people had already wilfully deserted God who merely left them to their own self-determination and self-destruction, part of the price of man's moral freedom." [6]

1. God Gave Them Up to Uncleanness (vv. 24–25)

With what result? Men dishonor their bodies and degrade them in lust. By so doing they try to change the truth of God into a lie. In other words, they forsake reality for unreality. This is a part of their vain reasonings; it actually is a part of their utter emptiness of understanding and folly of heart. When men violate God's purpose in sex, they make that which is holy to be unholy. Thus they serve the creature rather than the Creator. The philosophy of naturalism violates God's plan for life.

2. God Gave Them Up to Vile Affections (vv. 26–27)

More accurately, this phrase means "vile passions." Paul does not hide the truth. He has to declare the facts of life. Unregenerate men and women violate every standard of decency and propriety. They abandon all restraint. They practice unspeakable vices. Their practices are not only contrary to what is right but contrary to nature itself. As a result, they are "consumed by flaming passion for one another" (Williams). The Greek words used by Paul are not those for "men" and "women" but for "males" and "females." Thus they sink to the animal level—in reality, lower still, for their evil minds conceive unnatural ways to satisfy their lusts. And so they reap the harvest of their own corruption. They receive the full recompense of deception and wrongdoing. They are exposed to the inevitable wrath of God breaking forth from heaven.

3. *God Gave Them Up to a Reprobate Mind* (v. 28)

In this connection, Paul states again the essence of their iniquity or irreligion: "they refused to have God in their knowledge" (ASV). This means that they tried God and rejected him. He therefore abandoned them to a reprobate mind, or, as Lenski says, he "gave men up to a mind that acted the fool in moral matters."[7] Persisting in sin, they lost the capacity to distinguish between moral values and the ability to choose that which is right. When men are abandoned to a mind that is corrupted by vanity, lust, and falsehood—a mind utterly void of God and truth and right—they will do things which are not fitting. They will be controlled completely by their desires, desires which are either vicious or lustful or proud.

4. *Sin Is That Bad* (vv. 29-32)

There should be no surprise at the outcome of such a moral state. Men who have rejected God are the victims of their own iniquity. Paul closes his indictment with a catalogue of vices which portray the depths of moral ruin into which unregenerate men sink. Godless men always become unrighteous men. Perhaps the main point in Paul's long list is to emphasize the fact that the natural man will practice every kind of wrongdoing. The translation by Williams will help us to see something of the full force of Paul's indictment: "They overflow with every sort of evildoing, wickedness, greed, and malice; they are full of envy, murder, quarreling, deceit, ill-will; they are secret backbiters, open slanderers, hateful to God, insolent, haughty, boastful; inventors of new forms of evil, undutiful to parents, conscienceless, treacherous, with no human love or pity. Although they know full well God's sentence that those who practice such things deserve to die, yet they not only practice them but even applaud others who do them."

The unregenerate person is indeed worthy of death. He is guilty of sin, and the sentence of death has been pronounced against sin. He is under the condemnation of God because he is guilty in God's sight.

We have seen something of what sin is. It is as mean and as ugly and as degraded and as deadly as Paul described it to be. It "is an outside demonic power, alien to man's true (created) nature, which has gained entrance to man's life and has reduced him to bondage and made him a transgressor."[8] Sin is always the same, in every age, among all races, among all classes. And the wrath of God is always being revealed from heaven in judgment on all ungodliness and unrighteousness.

IV. THE PRINCIPLES OF GOD'S JUDGMENT—2:1–16

Paul now turns in his thinking to his own people, the Jews. They would have heartily approved his unmitigated condemnation of the Gentiles. But before coming directly to affirm the condemnation of the Jews under the wrath of God (2:17 to 3:8), Paul treats the principles of divine judgment.

Beginning with chapter 2, Paul adopts a dramatic form. He addresses an imaginary reader. But there is nothing imaginary in the ideas of this reader. He represents the claims and spirit of the Jews. He reflects their self-righteousness. He appears as a moralist, who is quick to condemn others but eager to excuse himself. He is in every way a counterpart of many others whose religion seems to consist chiefly in their readiness to find fault with other people.[9]

1. Useless to Make Excuse (v. 1)

Verse 1 has a direct connection with 1:18–32, as "therefore" indicates. The meaning of verse 1 is something like this: "The Gentiles are without excuse, and so are you, you who represent Jewish self-righteousness. You pose as a judge. You condemn the idolatry and vile wickedness of the Gentiles; but you, too, are guilty. You practice what you condemn, in principle if not in detail. You exercise the prerogative of moral evaluation, which shows you make moral distinctions; but you do not apply the same to yourselves, and so you have greater guilt." There are three principles by which God judges both Jews and Gentiles.

2. *God Judges According to Truth* (*vv. 2–5*)

The judgment of God is according to reality. It is according to what is right. It rests upon what God is and upon what man does. God does not deal with man on the basis of his race or his nationality or his social standing. God is true, and his judgment always rings true. On this basis the Jews could not expect favoritism. They could not expect God to be blind to their disobedience and unbelief. They had no right to expect God to judge others and not sit in judgment on them. It was utterly foolish for them to expect to "escape the judgment of God."

Actually, God had dealt with the Jews with unusual mercy, but this had placed them under greater obligation. The riches of God's goodness and forbearance and longsuffering had been bestowed on the Jews to a special degree, in keeping with God's purpose of redemption through them. This should have evoked humility and repentance. Instead, it caused them to feel that they were favorites, so that they became proud and presumptuous. They expected God to deal with the Gentiles in severity but to be easy on them, as two quotations from the Book of Wisdom indicate: "While therefore thou dost chasten us, thou scourgest our enemies ten thousand times more" (12:22); God judges the Jews with mercy; the heathen are "judged with wrath" (11:9). By their attitude the Jews had shown contempt for God's wonderful goodness toward them, never considering that the very purpose of God's mercy was to lead them to repentance.

Their hearts were hard and impenitent, when they should have been melted with godly sorrow. There will be fearful consequences, Paul says. God's judgment will be in keeping with truth, according to the reality of their unrepentant attitude. Therefore, the wrath of God will rest on the Jew as well as the Gentile. There will be an awful day of retribution. Here Paul declares the fact of a final day of judgment. The wrath of God is being constantly revealed against all iniquity, but, also, there will be a consummation in "the day of wrath and revelation of the righteous judgment of God."

Scarcely any truth in the Bible needs more emphasis today than the certain fact of divine judgment. The day of wrath is coming in which judgment will be meted out in keeping with truth and reality. God has done and God is doing his utmost to warn men and to cause them to repent. They ought to change their minds about him and change their ways in response to his long-suffering mercy. Self-righteousness and hardheartedness, no less than idolatry and unrestrained lust, will merit the wrath of righteous judgment.

3. *God Judges According to Deeds* (*vv. 6–11*)

This is the second principle stated by Paul. The Jews wanted to be judged on the basis of privilege, when God "will render to every man according to his deeds." Man is morally responsible, and therefore he will be judged according to what he does. The Jew could claim no advantage because he was the son of Abraham. He must stand on the same level as other men. In keeping with this principle, Paul says that those who earnestly seek for life will receive life. If with endurance marked by welldoing they strive for glory and honor and immortality, God will give them eternal life according to their deeds.

In contrast, for persons who are factious, who rebel against the truth and give themselves to unrighteousness, there shall be "indignation and wrath, tribulation and anguish." The Greek construction makes it clear that God does not "render" the rewards of iniquity as he "gives" eternal life to those seeking it. In other words, the reward for good deeds is a gift from God, but the reward for evil deeds is the infliction of wrath. God renders the verdict which matches the deed and the guilt. Paul repeats a part of the truth in verse 10, that is, he emphasizes the fact that the man who does good will receive "glory, honour, and peace." Whether one is a Jew or Gentile makes no difference. God's judgment is not affected by one's race but by his conduct. God is absolutely impartial—which is the meaning of "there is no respect of persons with God."

The question arises, Does not Paul here teach salvation by works? Emphatically no. Paul's words must be interpreted in their context. He is not discussing the matter of salvation at all. Instead, he is discussing the principles by which God judges all men. He declares the positive truth that God "will render to every man according to his deeds." He could not be just and judge men on any other basis. As a matter of fact, whoever earnestly seeks for the glory and honor and immortality of heaven will seek it in the way that God has provided, through faith in Jesus Christ. Further, no one can ever achieve the goodness acceptable to God apart from faith in Christ.

4. *God Judges According to Light (vv. 12–16)*

Those who sin without the law will perish without the law; and those who sin under the law will be judged by the law. The fact that the Gentiles do not have the Mosaic law or the revelation of Christianity will not excuse them. Neither will the fact that the Jews have the Mosaic law protect them. It is not hearing the law which makes one just in the sight of God but doing the requirements of the law.

Even the Gentiles have the law of conscience. In many instances they may respond to a constraint of conscience and do things which are required in the law given to the Jews. They thus prove that they have a law written in their hearts. This does not mean that the conscience is an accurate guide as to what is right or wrong, but it means that every man has inborn moral capacity, so that he has moral responsibility. The law written in the heart of man bears witness to him, either accusing or excusing him. His conscience makes him to know that he is answerable before God for what he does.

Therefore, men are judged according to the light they have, and this means that the Gentiles, not having the law, are subject to this principle of judgment. As Paul points out in 1:19–23, the Gentiles have abundant evidence of God, but they are not willing to recognize him as God.

The same truth applies to the Jews. They have the law and will be judged on the basis of the light it has made available to them.

Paul sums up the whole matter in verse 16. Ultimately, God will judge all men according to the truth of the gospel by Jesus Christ. He is the Judge of the living and the dead. He is the revelation of the truth of God and the righteousness of God and the criterion by which every man and his deeds must be judged. The principles of divine judgment are all summed up in the person of Jesus Christ. If men have accepted him, they will be justified in the sight of God; if they have not accepted him, they will be condemned to everlasting destruction from the presence of God.

V. THE JEWS ALSO CONDEMNED—2:17 to 3:8

Now Paul resumes the argument in 1:19–32 to show that the Jews as well as the Gentiles are condemned. He turns from "the Greek confidence in wisdom to the Jewish reliance on the Law." [10] Man's plight in sin is every man's plight, both Jew and Gentile. We will see three reasons stated by Paul why the Jews are under condemnation.

1. Profession Without Practice (2:17-24)

First, the Jews rely upon the law, but they do not practice it. The law was given to them, but they have not kept it. They hide behind it rather than demonstrate it. They put their dependence in the possession of the law without feeling an obligation to obey it. Paul points this out with severe frankness in verses 17–24.

The Jew, whom Paul addresses in verse 17, stands for all the Jews. They had great pride in their name. They relied upon the law. They boasted that they were worshipers of the true God. They were in a position of distinct advantage because through the law they were in a position to understand God's will, recognize moral standards, and choose the things which were right. Their superior opportunity made them the victims of overweening pride. With self-righteous confidence and a feeling of superiority over the heathen, the Jews considered themselves to be a guide for the blind, a light for those in spiritual ignorance, an instructor of the foolish, and a teacher of babes. All these were highly honored titles. They claimed a knowledge of the truth as revealed in the law. Such was the boast, if not of the Jews generally, at least of the Judaizers and the self-righteous Jewish moralists who looked down on Gentiles with much contempt.

Christians are subject to the same temptations that overtook the Jews. We have the gospel of Christ. We have a name of supreme honor. We can know the will of God, and we are expected to choose the ways of moral excellence. We claim to possess the truth that will give moral and spiritual direction to all the peoples of the world. The question is, Are we properly aware of the obligations growing out of our stewardship? It is not enough to be the possessors of true religion. We must be true examples of its redemptive power and moral principles.

The Jews claimed to be teachers of others but were not willing to teach themselves or learn their own lessons. They proclaimed the commandments of God but broke them with impunity. Paul mentions three specific matters: stealing, adultery, and robbing temples. The first two are in the area of man's severest and most universal temptations. The Ten Commandments forbid both. But knowing these commandments has never been able to fortify man adequately against breaking them. The Jews, as well as the Gentiles, stooped to the lowest level of moral degeneracy.

Jesus condemned the scribes and Pharisees for extortion and uncleanness and the grossest of sins. He said to the scribes and Pharisees who brought to him the woman taken in sin, "He that is without sin among you, let him first cast a stone at her" (John 8:7). The history of the children of Israel adds its condemning evidence. And other writings at the time of Paul can leave no doubt that the apostle was only too factual in exposing the sinfulness of Jews as well as Gentiles.

Paul's word about robbing temples was equally pertinent. Anything connected with an idol was abomination to the Jews. But in the Roman world the Jews were exposed to unlimited temptation to snatch some idol of gold or silver or something else from a temple and exploit it for gain. Remember that in writing to the Ephesians, Paul called the covetous man an idolater (5:5). Any association with idols was in reality the utter renunciation of Judaism.

Thus the Jews boasted about the law, but through their lawbreaking they dishonored God. With the result that the name of God was blasphemed among the Gentiles because of the moral failure of Judaism.

And the same sobering truth has frightening application to Christians now. The non-Christian world knows of our boast in Christianity. It knows of our profession, of commitment to the teachings of Christ, and so the people of the world expect a demonstration of integrity, purity, and unselfishness. Every failure to live up to the standards of Christian morality becomes occasion for blaspheming Christ on the part of a pagan world. The Christian faith suffers more from the unchristian conduct of Christians than from anything else.

2. *Purpose of Circumcision Missed* (2:25–29)

In the wake of Paul's indictment of moral failure, the question would arise in the Jewish mind, "Does not our circumcision give us some advantage? Does it not guarantee favor in the sight of God?" The rite of circumcision was given by God to the Jews for a high purpose. It was meant to be a sign of their faith in God and thus to be an incentive for faithfulness to God. By disobedience to the law the Jews turned their circumcision into actual uncircumcision. Thus they were actually no better than the pagans. In fact, Paul says that the uncircumcision or the pagan who demonstrates in his life the righteousness of the law is better than the Jew who transgresses the law. In other words, a good pagan will have better standing than a bad Jew. This is in line with what Jesus said about the people of Chorazin and Bethsaida: "It shall be more tolerable for Tyre and Sidon at the day of judgment, than for you" (Matt. 11:22). The one who is circumcised is under obligation to observe the whole law, according to Paul's word in Galatians 5:3.

A true Jew is not made such by physical circumcision. It must be spiritual. One is made a real Jew by the circumcision of the heart. The Jews, therefore, could not claim refuge under a ceremony or advantage because of the rite of circumcision. It takes more than a ritual or sacrament to obtain acceptance before God. The forms of religion are of no value unless they produce the fruits of religion. Rites and ordinances are important just to the degree that they express spiritual devotion.

We can learn from this word of Paul about the Jews the inward and spiritual character of true religion. It is first of all a matter of the heart, and then it must become a matter of behavior and attitude.

3. *Stewardship of Privilege Betrayed* (3:1–8)

In the third place, the Jews stood condemned because they had betrayed their stewardship of opportunity and privilege. Paul did not deny that the Jews were in a position of advantage. He did not disparage circumcision in its true purpose. Rather, he magnified the very distinct position of advantage occupied by the Jews. Specifically, the oracles of God had been entrusted to them. Paul may have had in mind the entire Scriptures of the Old Testament, though his thought may have been restricted just to the commands and promises of God to the Jews. At any rate, God had entrusted to them a special revelation of himself, which included the promises of the Messiah. But they betrayed their stewardship. The truth committed to them did not lead to faith. Even so, their lack of faith did not invalidate the faithfulness of God.

The words in verse 3 may be translated faith or faithfulness, but Paul likely means faithfulness. Though the Jews betrayed their stewardship—at least, many of them proved unfaithful—their unfaithfulness could not nullify the faithfulness of God. Instead, his faithfulness was shown the more clearly by their unfaithfulness.

Paul quotes a petition from David's great prayer in Psalm 51 to show that David felt that his sin served to bring into bolder relief the justice of God. God is never unfair, and he could not treat lightly either the unbelief or the unfaithfulness of those to whom he had entrusted the very oracles of truth and righteousness.

To this argument two very strong objections arise in the Jewish mind. They may be stated as follows: (1) If our wrongdoing serves to magnify God's righteousness, or if man's sin serves to increase God's glory, is it not unjust for God to execute judgment? Paul thought that to raise the question almost savored of blasphemy—hence, "I speak as a man." The answer is no. If it were not right, how could God judge the world? God must execute judgment, else there will be moral chaos.

(2) Why should we be judged as sinners if our sin redounds to God's glory? This question was the same in essence as the charge hurled against Paul by the Judaizers again and again: that, if salvation is by grace, people are encouraged to sin that grace may abound. The objection in the Jewish mind and the slanderous accusations of the Judaizers were absurd. Not even the people of the world would approve the idea, "let us do evil, that good

may come." Paul repudiates the idea with the declaration, "whose damnation is just." Dodd translates this, "such arguments are rightly condemned."[11] But almost certainly the "whose" refers to the slanderers. They merit nothing but condemnation. Lenski says that "'whose' refers to the persons and not merely to their slander."[12]

VI. ALL GUILTY BEFORE GOD—3:9–20

These verses constitute a summary or recapitulation of what Paul has been saying. The conclusion of the whole matter is: All are under sin. The apostle sums it up by saying, "We have before proved both Jews and Gentiles, that they are all under sin." The Jews are no better off than the pagans. They have had great advantage in having the law and in the superior opportunity entrusted to them. But they have broken the law and betrayed their stewardship and are therefore guilty. The Gentiles are without excuse because they have rejected the light available to them and have turned away from the clear evidences of God to idolatry and lust. Jews and Greeks alike are under the sway of sin.

Paul clinches the truth by various quotations from the Old Testament to show the perversity and universal guilt of men. It is a dark picture, but it is true to life. It is true to the history of Israel. It is true to the pagan world. It is true to the experience of humanity.

There is no one righteous in the sense that he conforms to the standard required by God. There is no one with spiritual understanding who listens to God and seeks after God. Universally, men have turned away from God, "turned every one to his own way" (Isa. 53:6). Therefore, they are unprofitable in the sight of God because they are out of harmony with his will. Not even one does good after a manner which is well pleasing to God.

So devoted to sin are men universally that their throat is like an open grave, which may mean emitting the odors of death or yawning to take in that which is dead. The tongue is given over to deceit. The poison of falsehood and criticism is under their lips. Their speech is full of cursing and bitterness. They are quick to commit murder. Therefore, destruction and misery result from their deeds. The ways of peace are strange to them. And all this frightful perversity of mind and heart, this depravity in wickedness, is due to the fact that "there is no fear of God before their eyes." The unregenerate man has no reverence for God, no respect for him as God, and therefore no delight in his will or his love.

Verses 19–20 are the reaffirmation and conclusion of all that Paul has been saying in this section. From a negative standpoint, he is saying that men cannot save themselves by their own works. The law was not given to shield men from the wrath of God but rather that "every mouth may be stopped" or silenced. "Let man be silent as to his own righteousness and his claim of advantage; let him rather confess that he is a sinner." [13] The law was given that men might have the knowledge of sin, that they might become aware of their own sinfulness. "By the deeds of the law there shall no flesh be justified in his sight."

We come back then to Paul's affirmation in 1:18: "The wrath of God is revealed from heaven against all ungodliness and unrighteousness of men, who hold the truth in unrighteousness." All men are guilty before God. Therefore, all are condemned and under wrath. If there is no fear of God in the heart, there will not be obedience to God in life. Ungodliness leads to unrighteousness. Both alike are the objects of God's holy wrath. The person who does not know God through faith in Jesus Christ stands before God in a state of condemnation. The plight of unregenerate humanity is the depravity of the moral nature. Man is utterly impotent to save himself. His supreme need is the redemption that is in Christ Jesus.

Let us sum up the truth about man's plight in sin: (1) Sin is a fact in human experience. There is perversity at the core of man's being. It brings man to the lowest state of moral degeneracy and spiritual rebellion. (2) Man is morally responsible. He has light which he has not followed, truth which he has not obeyed. (3) Man's plight is one of natural pride, moral ruin, and spiritual impotence. (4) The wrath of a righteous God is a fearful reality. Judgment is going on now, and it will continue to go on until a final day of wrath in the full revelation of the righteous judgment of God. But man's plight is not without hope—because of God's grace—as Paul passes on so quickly to declare in the next section of his letter.

---

[1] Dodd, *op. cit.*, p. 19

[2] R. C. H. Lenski, *The Interpretation of St. Paul's Epistle to the Romans* (Columbus: Wartburg Press, 1945), p. 91

[3] Charles R. Erdman, *The Epistle to the Romans* (Philadelphia: The Westminster Press, 1925, 1953), p. 34

[4] Nygren, *op. cit.*, p. 101

[5] Lenski, *op. cit.*, p. 107

[6] Robertson, *op. cit.*, p. 330

[7] Lenski, *op. cit.*, p. 118

[8] Knox, *op. cit.*, p. 369

[9] Erdman, *op. cit.*, p. 36

[10] Scott, *op. cit.*, p. 33

[11] Dodd, *op. cit.*, p. 46

[12] Lenski, *op. cit.*, p. 225

[13] Nygren, *op. cit.*, p. 142

3

The Divine Remedy

Romans 3:21 to 4:25

THIS is the good news of the gospel: God has provided the remedy for sin. This is the very heart of Paul's letter to the Romans.

This is the gospel which Paul had everywhere preached. It was the gospel he now longed to preach in Rome. In a special way and with a special sense of sacred obligation, he felt a stewardship of the gospel with respect to all men. And it was this gospel which he knew to be the power of God unto salvation. Paul had found it so in his own experience, and he had seen it confirmed on all levels of life and among all kinds of persons. The apostle was not blind to the terror of man's plight in sin. This fact made him all the more anxious to proclaim the divine remedy through the cross of Christ.

In the foregoing chapter we learned of the unrighteousness of men. In this chapter we will learn of the righteousness of God made available to men on the one condition of faith. Thus we come to the doctrine of justification by faith. This truth was a revolutionary concept in New Testament times. And it is just as much so today.

I. THE RIGHTEOUSNESS OF GOD—3:21-24

Since the fall of man in the beginning, the supreme problem has been how to get right with God. How can man get rid of sin and be acceptable in God's sight? At last a way is found—one way and one alone. It has been manifested in the gospel: it is "God's way of giving men right standing with Himself" (Williams).

1. A New Way of Righteousness (v. 21)

At this point Paul turns back to his theme in 1:17. A new kind of righteousness has been revealed. It is the righteousness of God by faith. Paul is quick to declare that this righteousness is wholly apart from the law. It cannot be had by law or attained by law. It therefore cuts straight across the pride of man, who is so prone to think that he can do something of himself to get right with God. He is forever tempted to seek the righteousness of works. Nothing about the law can help him, except to acquaint him with his own sin. God requires righteousness, but he himself provides it.

This truth is made abundantly clear "by the law and the prophets," that is, by the Old Testament. Again and again the Old Testament Scriptures bear their witness to Christ. The gospel does not destroy the Old Testament; it simply fulfils it. And it is this witness of the law and the prophets that Paul now proclaims in the light of the coming of Jesus.

2. Available to All by Faith (vv. 22-23)

The righteousness of God is received by faith. It is a free gift, as we shall see later. The one condition is faith in Jesus Christ. Not belief about him or admiration for him, but faith in him is prerequisite to salvation. If faith has the right object, it will bring real righteousness. Men cannot earn it or deserve it, but they can receive it "by faith." It is for everyone who will believe.

There is no distinction between individuals or classes. The righteousness of God is available to Jews and Gentiles on the same terms. This means that race is not a factor in gaining acceptance with God. Neither is social standing or economic condition or moral respectability or cultural advantage. Paul has shown that there is no distinction from the standpoint of wrath and condemnation—both Jews and Gentiles are condemned. He now shows that there is no difference from the standpoint of righteousness and justification—it is for everyone who will believe.

The truth already set forth about the universal guilt of

all men under sin (1:18 to 3:20) is reaffirmed in verse 23: "All have sinned, and come short of the glory of God." This emphasizes the fact that the righteousness of God is offered to sinful, undeserving men. It must, therefore, be a free gift. Paul leaves absolutely no doubt about the universality of sin. Men have missed the mark, have come short of God's glory. The latter clause of the verse may be taken as a definition of sin. It means, according to Lenski, that men come short of the "praise from God." [1] Surely it means more than that. Men come short of God's purpose and demand. They have rebelled against his goodness and sovereignty. They come far short of likeness to him and reverence for him. They are thus guilty before him.

3. *Provided by Grace* (*v. 24*)

But God has found the way to help the man condemned in sin. The divine remedy is justification, grace, redemption. Our souls should break forth with praise and joy. These words should not be thought of as theological abstractions but as spiritual realities pregnant with the deepest meaning. To be justified means to be declared righteous in the sight of God, to be counted righteous. It does not mean that one is righteous, but he is declared to be right before God. The guilty one is treated as though he were no longer guilty.

Grace means the unmerited favor of God. It is one of the sublimest words in the Christian gospel. On the basis of grace, guilty sinners can be declared not guilty. It is amazing grace, indeed, on the part of God that provides pardon. Justification is all of grace, gratuitous and free, without merit or desert on man's part.

Redemption points to the ransom provided in Christ Jesus. This is a word about which the theologians have written much. It is one about which Christians need clear insight and profound appreciation. Its basic idea is ransom, or the price paid for the liberation of a slave. Therefore, it connotes deliverance or emancipation. Its major idea is not the payment of a price but simply emancipation. Thus, as

Paul uses it, it has the marvelous meaning of deliverance from the bondage of sin. Already the apostle had written to the Galatians, "Christ hath redeemed us from the curse of the law, being made a curse for us" (3:13). Jesus himself had said that "the Son of man came ... to give his life a ransom for many" (Mark 10:45). To sum up, "Anybody may have right standing with God as a free gift of His undeserved favor, through the ransom provided in Christ Jesus" (Williams).

Every idea in verse 24 emphasizes that God is doing something for us which we cannot do for ourselves. He is the one who gives us a right standing in spite of our guilt. He does it freely, voluntarily, generously. It is all a matter of grace. It has come through the redemption in Jesus Christ. Salvation can be found in no other, for he alone is the ransom, and he alone can set us free from sin.

It is important to note the form of "being justified." It describes repeated action, which means each person individually is being set right before God.[2] The divine remedy for sin makes possible a new status before God on the part of the sinner—"from condemnation to acquittal, from bondage to freedom, from guilt to innocence."[3]

II. PROPITIATION THROUGH THE CROSS—3:25-26

If what Paul has just said is true, does it mean that God is careless about sin? Does he mean to imply that the righteousness of God can be imputed to guilty sinners as a matter of course? How can the righteousness of God be received by faith, purely on the grounds of God's grace, without undermining the very justice of God in a moral universe? What Paul sets forth in verses 25-26 answers these questions and gives us the key to what precedes.

1. Atonement Made

God has done something. He has done something eternal and supreme. He has provided a propitiation for the sins of the world.

At this point we need to consider the meaning of "propitiation." Biblical scholars are by no means agreed as to its meaning. There are some who claim that propitiation implies that God is angry with men and that his anger must be appeased. And so they reject the idea of propitiation as being out of keeping with God's nature as perfect love. Although the word for propitiation is derived from a Greek word which pagan writers used to express placating the anger of a man or a god, it does not have to have that specific connotation here. It must be interpreted in harmony with the nature of God. On the other hand, it cannot be properly interpreted out of harmony with the context of these verses.

C. H. Dodd takes the position that propitiation really means expiation: God "puts forward the means whereby the guilt of sin is removed, by sending Christ."[4] Other scholars—Nygren and Lenski—put strong emphasis upon the fact that *hilasterion,* the word for propitiation, is used in the New Testament only here and in Hebrews 9:5 where it obviously means the mercy seat.[5, 6] They also call attention to the customary use of this word in the Septuagint for mercy seat. Therefore, they insist that God did set forth Christ as the mercy seat, or the covering of the mercy seat. Hence, "in Christ God reveals himself in His glory. Now He does not, as before, hide it behind a cloud of incense in the Holy of Holies. On the contrary, He has now put Christ forward before all the world as our *hilasterion,* our mercy seat."[7]

We are content to take sides with the more traditional view that the word used by Paul is properly translated "propitiation." A. T. Robertson quotes Deissmann about this verse as follows: "The crucified Christ is the votive gift of the Divine Love for the salvation of men."[8] Then Robertson continues, "God gave his Son as the means of propitiation."[9] This does not need to carry with it any concept of an angry God bent on retribution. It does not even remotely suggest that God has to be induced to love sinners. God did not have to placate anger, but he did have to make a propitiatory offering for sin to satisfy the demands of his own justice. He had to act in keeping with the seriousness of sin and his own righteous wrath against all ungodliness and all unrighteousness. God had to act in keeping with the demands of his own moral nature in a moral universe. As Robertson says, "God demanded the atonement and provided it."[10]

Verse 25 points to a mighty act in history. God did set forth for himself a propitiatory offering in the death of Jesus Christ on the cross. He was publicly offered for sin, before God and before the world. By that sacrifice of reconciliation, offered once for all, God provided the means by which sin is forgiven. The propitiation was made possible by the shed blood of Christ. Its blessing is made available to us by faith.

2. Righteousness Demonstrated

God provided propitiation through the cross to satisfy the demands of his justice "because of the passing over of the sins done aforetime, in the forbearance of God; for the showing, . . . of his righteousness at this present season: that he might himself be just, and the justifier of him that hath faith in Jesus" (ASV). There is no reason to shy away from the truth Paul affirmed. If the condemnation for sin is as serious as it is shown to be in 1:18 to 3:20, then nothing less than propitiation through the cross can provide pardon. If the counterpart of the righteousness of God is the wrath of God, then there had to be provision through the blood of Christ for the atonement of sin.

During Old Testament times there was a passing over of sins done aforetime—a better translation than "the remission of sins that are past"—and judgment was withheld through the forbearance of God. Even during Old Testament times faith was counted for righteousness before the propitiation was actually made. Christ was the propitiation for all sins—past, present, and future—even the sin of the world. Because he suffered vicariously in man's stead, God can be absolutely just; and he can also justify the one who has faith in Jesus.

3. Forgiveness Justified

Paul faced the awful reality of sin. He declared the redemptive act of God through Christ on the cross by means of which divine grace is revealed and divine justice demonstrated. He proclaimed the wondrous truth that through the crucified and risen Christ we have redemption and reconciliation. It is because of the propitiation through the cross that divine forgiveness is justified.

Some commentators insist that the righteousness of God in verses 25–26 is exactly the same in meaning as in verse 21—the idea being that God was showing his righteousness available for man's justification rather than satisfying the demands of his own justice. But to take this position does not answer several problems—the moral nature of God, the necessity for atonement, the passing over of sins before the coming of Christ, and the clear implication in verse 26. Also, the Greek form in the last part of verse 26 indicates purpose. God did something "that he himself might be just and the justifier of the one who has faith in Jesus." This is the key phrase which establishes the connection between the righteousness of God and the righteousness by faith.[11] "Nowhere has Paul put the problem of God more acutely or profoundly. . . . God's mercy would not allow him to leave man to his fate. God's justice demanded some punishment for sin." [12]

Let us not fail to observe that the cross of Christ is central in the gospel according to Paul. It is the heartbeat of the Christian faith. It is the divine achievement for the salvation of a lost world. The cross, in reality, is a spiritual Mount Everest that towers in majesty and sublimity above every other peak in the revelation of truth.

III. JUSTIFICATION BY FAITH—3:27–31

Paul can now come to his conclusion: We are justified by faith and faith alone. This is one of the foremost doctrines of his letter, one of the foremost teachings of Christianity. Three very important truths are emphasized.

1. Boasting Is Excluded (v. 27)

If salvation could be achieved by the law or works, men would have a right to boast. This concept makes a strong appeal to man's pride. It was so with the Jews; it is so with many people who profess to be Christians. They are determined to try to do something to save themselves. They insist that they are honest and charitable, or that they belong to a church, or that they are as good as other people. All of which is boasting and depending on self rather than Christ.

Paul could claim that his zeal for the religion of the fathers outstripped any of his own age (Gal. 1:14). He could claim moral excellence to the highest degree and absolute conformity to the legal requirements of the law (Phil. 3:6). But for salvation he claimed no righteousness of his own, that by the law, but the righteousness of God by faith (Phil. 3:9). This is what Paul is insisting on here in his letter to the Romans, that justification by faith makes boasting impossible.

The law of works will not work to gain salvation, but the law of faith will work to receive salvation. The law of faith is in harmony with both God and man. It claims God's free grace, and it recognizes man's guilt and helplessness.

2. Faith Alone Is Necessary (v. 28)

"Therefore we conclude that a man is justified by faith without the deeds of the law." Luther translated this "by faith alone." That is exactly what Paul means. Nothing else needs to be added to faith and nothing else can be added to faith—if we understand faith in its true meaning or very essence, namely, voluntary commitment to Christ in penitence for sin and in humble acceptance of him as Saviour and Lord. God has provided the remedy freely, as a matter of grace. We do not have to deserve it, we never could deserve it. We do not receive it through an ordinance such as baptism. It can never be received through a sacrament such as the mass. It can never be received through joining a church or doing good deeds or repeating prayers or confessing creeds. If men would only listen to the clear words of the Scriptures! The only way for sinful man to be justified in the sight of God is by faith and faith alone.

3. *God Is Concerned for All Men* (*vv. 29–31*)

Justification by faith affirms God's concern for all men. He is not the God of the Jews only, but the God of Gentiles as well. He is the God of all races and all nations. His love is all-inclusive. Christ tasted death for every man. God deals with all alike. Therefore, faith is the source of justification for the circumcised and the agency of justification for the uncircumcised. God does not have one plan of salvation for those who know the gospel and another plan for those who do not. The divine remedy is for all men on the same terms, through faith in Jesus Christ.

Paul adds a sort of postscript, lest someone misunderstand what he has said. Justification by faith does not make the law of no effect. The law is not made null and void; instead it is established. Jesus said, "Think not that I am come to destroy the law, or the prophets: I am not come to destroy, but to fulfil" (Matt. 5:17). The law was never meant to be the way of salvation. "By the law is the knowledge of sin." The Christian strives to live by the moral requirements of the law. In the teaching of Christ the standards of the law find their true interpretation, and in the power of Christ men find their strength to live according to those standards before the world.

IV. AN ILLUSTRATION OF SAVING FAITH—4:1–25

To clinch his argument, Paul now turns to a telling illustration from the Old Testament. He turns to Abraham as an example of the truth of the gospel. The force of his illustration grows out of the fact that Abraham was the ideal in the Jewish mind. He represented the best in Judaism. All the Jews revered him as the father of their nation.

The covenant with Israel was first made with Abraham.

Also, in the Jewish mind, Abraham was a type of righteousness through the law. Paul, therefore, uses the strongest illustration he could possibly choose to show that, contrary to Jewish thinking, Abraham was not an example of righteousness by the law but an illustration of justification by faith. Abraham had gained acceptance before God, not by works, but by faith.

1. Righteousness Not by Law but by Faith (vv. 1–8)

There are variations in the Greek text in verse 1. Without arguing different viewpoints, we suggest the following translation: "What then shall we say about Abraham, our forefather according to the flesh?" Paul's question is likely rhetorical. What light can we get about this matter from Abraham? How was he made right in the sight of God? If he was justified by works, as the Jews thought, he would have ground for boasting. Paul is quick to add, "not before God." Actually, he was not justified by works, as the Scriptures so clearly prove. Long before the law was given, "Abraham believed God, and it was counted unto him for righteousness"—as we find also in Genesis 15:6. When one earns a reward, he receives it as the payment of a debt, not as a matter of grace. But if one does not work, any reward received is a gift. That is exactly the case with the Christian. He believes on the One who justifies the ungodly, so that "his faith is counted for righteousness."

This truth in verse 5 is central in the gospel. God forgives ungodly men on the simple condition of faith. In that forgiveness there is unmeasured blessedness, as David's experience and testimony so strongly confirm. David committed great sin. He came to know the supreme blessing of forgiveness, not because he had not committed sin, but because God no longer imputed sin to him or reckoned him guilty of sin. Paul's point is that Abraham could not be claimed as an example of justification by the works of the law, for the Scriptures specifically say that on the basis of his faith righteousness was imputed to him.

2. Righteousness Not Dependent on Circumcision (vv. 9–12)

The Jews of course felt that there was distinct advantage in circumcision. But Paul says the blessedness of a right standing with God or acceptance before God applies not only to the circumcised but the uncircumcised as well. The proof is again found in Abraham, for his faith was reckoned for righteousness before the rite of circumcision was instituted. One needs only to turn back to Genesis 15 and then to Genesis 17 to verify this point and also to learn that the rite of circumcision was given as a seal and sign of the covenant already established with Abraham. This very meaningful rite, then, was never meant to be a shield behind which to hide or an advantage about which to boast, but it was meant to be a testimony of faith and the sign of a covenant relationship existing between God and his people.

In other words, for Abraham circumcision was simply a seal of the righteousness by faith. Thus, in the true sense Abraham is "the father of all them that believe," whether circumcised or uncircumcised, whether Jew or Gentile. The one thing that matters is true faith. Paul is declaring that the righteousness of God has nothing at all to do with an external rite or a religious ceremony. It is a matter of the heart. The outward act is to be a declaration of an inner experience and attitude. The apostle is also declaring another truth of tremendous import. The true children of Abraham are not his seed according to the flesh but those who have exercised saving faith by which the righteousness of God is imputed to them.

3. The Promise Not Conditioned on Law (vv. 13–22)

This means really that the promise made to Abraham was one of grace. The covenant was made hundreds of years before the law was given. There could not possibly be, therefore, anything about the promise dependent upon the law. Inasmuch as the one condition was faith, the promise made to Abraham would include all who have the same kind of faith.

Again in verse 16 Paul states that Abraham "is the father of us all." By this he means that Christians claim Abraham as their forefather also, not according to the flesh but according to faith. The Jews had no peculiar grounds for boasting that they were the children of Abraham. In fact, apart from his kind of faith they had no right to claim to be his children at all. God promised Abraham that in him all the families of the earth would be blessed. If we can claim kinship with him in the faith which is reckoned for righteousness, we can also claim the heritage of God's promise as we humbly accept the stewardship of God's purpose.

In connection with this argument that the promise made to Abraham was not through the law but through the righteousness of faith, Paul helps us to understand something of what faith is and how it works. Faith claims a promise and acts on it in spite of conditions which seem to make its fulfilment impossible. God promised Abraham that he would be the father of many nations. But both Abraham and Sarah were old in years. They had no children. How could Abraham become the father of many nations? He faced the fact that from a natural standpoint Sarah could not give birth to children, but "he staggered not at the promise of God through unbelief." He believed that God could do what he had promised, that God could quicken that which was dead, that he could give them children in spite of their age and thus bring to realization numberless seed. Paul's conclusion in verse 22 is as strong as he could make it: his faith was credited for righteousness.

All through the chapter Paul has repeatedly declared that Abraham's faith was reckoned for righteousness. He is talking about the faith which brings one into right standing before God. He is talking about saving faith, that receives from God what one does not deserve, justification in spite of sin, because God justifies "freely by his grace through the redemption that is in Christ Jesus."

4. Instruction to Christians (vv. 23-25)

The last three verses of the chapter point out the fact that the illustration of Abraham gives instruction to Christians. The record about Abraham's faith was not preserved for his sake alone, but for us also. We are to have the same kind of faith that Abraham did, one related to death and resurrection. The difference is that Abraham's faith looked forward; our faith is fixed in Jesus Christ, who died but who, by the power of God, was raised up from the dead and who is our living Lord and Saviour. He was delivered up to crucifixion for our trespasses, and he was raised "for our justification." Paul means "with a view to our justification."[13] The death and resurrection of Christ are one sublime redemptive act for the redemption of men.

There is a divine remedy for sin. God has provided redemption. He has set forth Jesus Christ to be the propitiation for sin. There is one condition, and one alone, whereby the divine remedy is received—faith in Jesus Christ. The doctrine of justification by faith means that we are given right standing before God, not through merit, not through the works of the law, not by rite or ceremony, but by faith in him who is our Saviour and Lord.

---

[1] Lenski, *op. cit.*, p. 249

[2] Robertson, *op. cit.*, p. 347

[3] Dodd, *op. cit.*, p. 57

[4] *Ibid.*, p. 55

[5] Nygren, *op. cit.*, p. 156

[6] Lenski, *op. cit.*, p. 258

[7] Nygren, *op. cit.*, p. 158

[8] Robertson, *op. cit.*, pp. 347–348

[9] *Ibid.*

[10] *Ibid.*

[11] William Sanday and Arthur C. Headlam, *The Epistle to the Romans*, "The International Critical Commentary" (New York: Charles Scribner's Sons, 1926), p. 90

[12] Robertson, *op. cit.*, p. 348

[13] *Ibid.*, p. 354

4

Saved by Grace

Romans 5:1-21

LET US remind ourselves that the theme of Paul's letter is the righteousness of God. The apostle has presented two major aspects of this theme: First, man is desperately in need of God's righteousness because of his sin; second, God has provided righteousness which is available through faith in Jesus Christ.

Having shown so conclusively that man is justified by faith and faith alone, the apostle would, it seems, naturally turn at this point to deal with the second aspect of the righteousness of God in Christian sanctification. And thus many of the commentators outline the letter to the Romans and place chapter 5 in the section 5:1 to 8:39. Others make chapter 5 a part of their treatment of justification and so encompass it in the section 1:18 to 5:21. At any rate, all agree that this chapter offers real difficulty in interpretation.

For our purposes it has seemed better to treat chapter 5 separately. It is not actually a part of the argument about justification, which is concluded with the illustration in chapter 4. Neither is it properly, except the first five verses, a treatment of the saved life of the believer. This chapter seems rather a connecting link, pointing both backward and forward. It is a transition which reaffirms and emphasizes the truths already presented and which prepares the way for a richer understanding of the new life in Christ.

Paul's first thought in this chapter is the blessedness of the salvation in Christ (vv. 1–5). Then he thinks of how this salvation has been made possible by God's redeeming love (vv. 6–11). Following this he interprets, by way of the contrast between Adam and Christ, the nature and scope of this wonderful salvation (vv. 12–21). One idea more than any other seems to gather up the profound truth in this chapter, namely, we are saved by grace. If we miss this truth, we shall never understand the gospel according to Paul. If we learn this truth, we shall grasp the most essential truth in the doctrine of salvation.

I. THE BLESSEDNESS OF SALVATION—5:1–5

As suggested before, it seems natural for Paul to begin his treatment of what the righteousness of God will mean in the Christian's life or to set forth the fruits of justification. This is what he does on an inspiring level in these five verses. There are four major aspects of this blessedness, as we shall now see.

1. Peace (vv. 1–2a)

First of all, the Christian has peace. Because by faith he has been declared righteous in the sight of God, the Christian is free from the wrath of God. Also, because he has been reconciled, the Christian is no longer hostile toward God. He knows the inner peace of forgiveness; but, better still, he stands in a peaceful relationship with God.

But the heart of what Paul says is, "let us have peace" or "let us keep on enjoying peace." The scholars differ about the form of the Greek word translated "we have," but the best evidence supports the form meaning "let us have." This is the very point that Paul wants to stress—we ought to enjoy to the full the peace with God which has come "through our Lord Jesus Christ." There can be no peace apart from him, no peace apart from justification by faith. This peace passes all understanding. The burden of guilt is gone. We can forever rejoice in the fact that God's righteousness is imputed to us; our sins have been forgiven.

Also, we have access by faith into a new status, the status of grace. That, too, has come through Christ as our

Saviour. One thinks naturally of the word in Hebrews, "Let us therefore come boldly unto the throne of grace" (4:16), because we have access through Jesus Christ, our great High Priest. Our standing before God is a gift of grace. Our access is by faith. The blessed result is peace and confidence.

2. Hope (v. 2b)

We can "rejoice in hope of the glory of God." But the meaning is, "let us continue boasting or exulting in hope of the glory of God." This is not the boasting of the legalist or the self-righteous person. It is rather the exultation of the saved person who knows that salvation is by grace. Hope itself is one of the greatest of blessings. Paul puts it along with "faith" and "love" as the values and virtues of greatest worth. Hope, of course, takes on its highest and truest meaning when it is Christian hope. That means that it has assurance and certainty, that its object is God and the consummation of his kingdom. In this passage Paul makes it very personal. Because of justification by faith, we are to continue exulting in hope of the glory in God, certain that we shall share in that glory in the life to come. Again, the truth ought to be impressed upon us that the Christian's supreme joys are not material pleasures and fleshly satisfactions but the blessedness of spiritual peace and hope.

3. Joy in Tribulation (vv. 3–5a)

We have the same word and the same form with respect to tribulation that we do with respect to hope. Therefore, we are to boast or glory or exult in tribulations. No one but a Christian can do this, in the true sense. There is nothing in this of a martyr complex. Paul is simply facing the facts of Christian experience. Tribulation is a part of life. Suffering in some form and to some degree is inevitable. Added to this, tribulation or suffering is a part of the cross-bearing of Christian discipleship. It is a part of what is sure to result from a faithful witness in a world of evil.

A part of the blessedness of salvation is a new concept of suffering and a new outlook on life. We have new insight into the values of suffering, new strength to endure suffering, and new willingness to face the necessity for suffering. We learn that tribulation, rightly borne, produces patience or endurance; endurance will produce something tested and approved; such tested character will serve to increase our hope; and this kind of hope will never disappoint us or deceive us or put us to shame.

What is Paul saying? Simply this: Christians can have joy in suffering because they see it as a necessary part of life, because they themselves are related to the will of a loving God, because they have grace sufficient to bear suffering, and because they know that it can turn out to the development of a nobler and stronger character. It can create a stronger hope of "the glory which shall be revealed in us" in the life to come.

4. Hearts Full of Love (v. 5b)

This is the climax of all blessedness: "The love of God is shed abroad in our hearts." Williams' translation gives us a gripping picture: "God's love has flooded our hearts." The agent is the Holy Spirit. By means of his work and through his very presence, the divine love fills our beings.

All the persons of the Trinity have a part in our salvation. God justifies us because of faith. His righteousness is made possible because of the redemption of Christ. The Holy Spirit makes us aware of our need, enables us to exercise faith, and floods our hearts with God's love. He himself is the Spirit of love, and his presence means a heart flooded with love.

The love of God satisfies the yearning of the heart or answers the longing of the heart. The soul is restless until it finds peace with God. The love of God transforms the heart. It conquers enmity and rebellion and ingratitude. The love of God restores the heart with new life. It cleanses the heart of all sin. It fills the heart with goodness and truth.

II. Reconciliation Through Christ—5:6–11

These verses paint a picture of redemptive love that the world knows nothing about apart from the gospel of Jesus Christ. Here Paul declares that the basis for salvation by grace is God's love for sinners and the reconciliation effected by the death of Christ. God's love is the explanation of our salvation. While we can never with our mortal minds sound the depths or grasp the full dimensions of God's love, let us seek to explore the way in which his love has provided salvation by grace for sinful men. Perhaps the more helpful approach will be, not a verse by verse analysis, but a consideration of the essential truths set forth.

1. God's Redeeming Love

The first truth declared by Paul is that nothing on our part justifies what Christ did for us. Nothing on our part could merit God's love or Christ's sacrifice. "We were yet without strength." This means that we were weak and helpless. "We were yet sinners." This means that we had missed the mark in life and had come short of doing God's will. "We were enemies." This means that we were hostile toward God, rebellious, self-willed, set against his righteous will and sovereign rule. Paul could not set forth this indictment against lost people without including himself. He was frightfully conscious of his own former condition in the bondage and guilt of sin.

In spite of our helplessness and sinfulness and ungodliness, God loves us. There is no way to explain God's love but by God himself. It is his nature to love. His whole being reaches out with desire and compassion and infinite good will toward every person in all the earth. No one is so wicked, no one so corrupt, no one so violent or adulterous, no one so depraved or morally destitute, but that God's love reaches him and encompasses him and offers the riches of grace to him.

Another truth is that God's redeeming love found expression in Christ's death for ungodly men. The essence of the gospel is this: "But God commendeth his love toward us, in that, while we were yet sinners, Christ died for us." John declared the same matchless truth. "Herein is love, not that we loved God, but that he loved us, and sent his Son to be the propitiation for our sins" (1 John 4:10).

We thus come to understand what grace is. Divine love is the source of divine grace. God has done something for all mankind which no man in all the earth ever deserved. We are saved by grace because we are saved through no merit that could occasion God's love or justify his redemption. Love took the initiative in providing a sacrifice for sin. Therefore, salvation has its beginning in God's initiative as he declares his love, offers his forgiveness, and seeks to bring sinners to an awareness of their need and to an acceptance of his mercy. We know this to be true because "God commendeth his love toward us, in that, while we were yet sinners, Christ died for us." God has shown his love in this way, proved his love to this degree, and shared his love at this cost.

God's redeeming love is altogether above the human level—infinitely beyond it and above it! Paul makes this clear by the contrast between Christ's death for ungodly ones and man's willingness to sacrifice for others. "Scarcely for a righteous man will one die." That is, hardly anyone would be willing to die for another man who is just and upright. Some few, perhaps, would dare to die for a person of outstanding goodness. Man's concern and good will for other men is scarcely ever marked by sacrifice to the point of death. But when it is, it is always for one who is righteous or one who is marked by superior goodness. It never becomes sacrificial for the unworthy and ungodly or for those who are enemies.

But God's love is just like that. It includes the worst and lowest, the most destitute and most corrupt. It includes those who have insulted God's holiness and disobeyed his commandments and spurned his mercy. God commends his love toward sinners. How conscious Paul must have been of the amazing love of God in Christ that reached even to him, though he made havoc of the church and persecuted the saints even to death. How conscious we ought to be of the amazing grace by which we have been saved through faith!

2. *Christ's Vicarious Death*

The next great truth here presented is, "Christ died for us." Five times in these six verses Paul affirms the fact of Christ's death: He "died for the ungodly"; he "died for us"; "being now justified by his blood"; "we were reconciled to God by the death of his Son"; "by whom we have now received the reconciliation." All this repeats what Paul says in 3:24–25. The death of Christ was an event in history. It was the redemptive act of the almighty God. It was a propitiation for sin. It was the supreme demonstration of God's love. It was the achievement of divine wisdom and grace. It was the victory of divine righteousness.

Another aspect of Christ's death is stated as clearly as language can make it. Paul says that Christ's death was vicarious. He "died *for* the ungodly"; he "died *for* us." In both instances Paul uses a preposition which denotes "in behalf" or "instead of." We can never understand the cross apart from this concept of Christ's sacrifice.

It is true that some theologians and many other persons stumble over the vicarious concept of Christ's death. They claim that it involves a conflict in the Godhead, that it makes Christ the victim of God's wrath, and that it implies a view of the righteousness and severity of God out of keeping with his nature as infinite love.

Some observations may be made in reply: (1) As we think of the death of Christ, we must keep in mind the unity of the Godhead. The Father, the Son, and the Spirit shared the redemptive concern and the redemptive purpose. In a very real way, beyond human comprehension, they shared the experience of redemptive suffering. (2) Christ was in no sense a victim of God's wrath against sin. He shared God's wrath against sin and freely offered himself to bear the full consequences of sin in order to make atonement for sin. (3) The cross does not contradict the nature of God as perfect love; it rather proves and demonstrates God's nature as love, holy and infinite love. The cross shows how far God would go in love for lost men to save them from sin.

The Pauline view of the cross—a view in perfect harmony with Christ's own view of his death—recognizes the gravity of sin and the righteousness and love of God. Nothing short of a vicarious sacrifice, innocent and holy, eternal and divine, could make atonement for sin.

As our ransom, Christ redeems and delivers us from sin; and thus we learn something of the cost of our salvation. As our substitute, Christ bears the punishment for sin; and thus we receive justification and forgiveness not by merit but by grace through faith. As our atonement, Christ reconciles us to God; we are made nigh by the cross.

The cross is more than a theory, more than an example, more than a principle. It was an event in history, when the Son of God died for mankind. It is a propitiation for sin, so that God can justify all who believe in Jesus. The truth was affirmed by Paul that Christ suffered in our stead and bore the penalty of death on our behalf. We are saved by grace because Christ died for us. We do, indeed, have "redemption through his blood, the forgiveness of sins, according to the riches of his grace" (Eph. 1:7).

Let us never misunderstand Christ's death by thinking it was forced upon him. He died voluntarily for all sinners. His own word confirms that: "I am the good shepherd: ... and I lay down my life for the sheep.... No man taketh it from me, but I lay it down of myself. I have power to lay it down, and I have power to take it again. This commandment have I received of my Father" (John 10:11–18). Christ was one with the Father in redemptive love, in redemptive purpose, in redemptive sacrifice, and in redemptive power. He so loved the world that he gave his own life for ungodly ones—for us and for all men.

We are reminded in verse 9 that "being now justified by his blood, we shall be saved from wrath through him." In other words, we have no occasion to fear the revelation of the wrath of God in the day of judgment. Through Christ we are delivered from the wrath to come (1 Thess. 1:10).

3. *The Christian's Confidence and Praise*

The final truth set forth in connection with God's saving grace declares that "we were reconciled to God by the death of his Son." We were enemies, or hostile toward God. Reconciliation was not needed to change God's attitude toward sinful men but to change their feeling toward God. By the death of Jesus we are made aware of God's friendliness, God's love, God's yearning to forgive.

Paul goes on to emphasize the fact that since we have been reconciled by Christ's death, "we shall be saved by his life." We are brought into a right status before God by virtue of the sacrifice of the cross, but we are saved by faith in a living Saviour. Our salvation is due to the indwelling presence of the living Christ. In this word of the apostle there is also emphasis upon the continuance and consummation of salvation. It began with justification by faith. It continues through sanctification in the power of the Spirit. It will be consummated in the glorification of eternity. It is of utmost importance that we understand salvation in terms of a vital relation with our living Saviour. Christ lives in us. On this ground we can be confident.

In verse 11 we have a sort of summary, conclusion, and climax. On the basis of our salvation, "we keep on boasting in God through our Lord Jesus Christ." This is the meaning of Paul's word rather than "joy." Because we are saved by grace, we have no reason for exulting in ourselves. We can have no pride in achieving our own salvation. We must attribute it all to God through Christ. We have occasion for endless praise and continuous thanksgiving and unmeasured gratitude because of God's redeeming love.

III. SALVATION BY GRACE INTERPRETED—5:12–21

This is one of the most difficult of all the passages in Paul's letter. The commentators differ in their opinions about how these verses fit into Paul's major argument. Let us approach them with humility of spirit, fully aware that Paul's thought is often hard to comprehend. Also, it is important to concentrate attention upon the major ideas or central truths in this passage. We shall not be able to resolve all the problems or answer all the questions that come to our minds. The major truths are clear enough and are of greatest importance.

Often this passage is conceived as a contrast between Adam and Christ. Actually, it deals chiefly with Christ. Adam, the head of the human race, serves as an illustration to make more impressive what Christ has done for the redemption of men. Paul's major purpose is to stress the universality of sin and the supremacy of grace. In a sense, the apostle looks backward to reaffirm all that he has said about man's plight in sin and what he has said about the divine provision of salvation. Throughout there is an implied emphasis on the centrality of justification, and there is the strongest possible emphasis on the sufficiency of grace. Realizing that the passage is "pregnant with mystery," let us now look at it more closely.

The "wherefore" or "therefore" with which Paul begins seems to point back to the argument in verses 6–11, unless it be to all that has preceded.

1. *The Universality of Sin (vv. 12–14)*

First of all, we are faced with the universality of sin. Sin entered into the world through the fall, through Adam's disobedience. Paul does not try to go back beyond this point in accounting for the tragic fact of sin. The penalty for sin was death. The whole race was affected in that it suffered moral contamination at its source. Inasmuch as "all have sinned," the consequences of sin or death "passed upon all men" or "passed through to all men." In a very real sense, which defies understanding and explanation, man inherits a sinful nature. It has a bent toward sin, which breaks out in conscious acts of sin when one matures to the point of moral responsibility. Wherever you find human nature, through all generations, in all the world, you find sin.

This ought forever to correct the concept that human nature is inherently good, that men by nature are children of God in the true sense, or that one can grow up into the kingdom of God without ever having had a consciousness of being lost and condemned. Paul's word here corresponds exactly with what he wrote to the Ephesians: we "were by nature the children of wrath" (2:3). The inclination toward sin does not first of all produce hatred for sin but rather love for sin and, as a consequence, guilt because of sin as soon as one becomes old enough to be morally competent or morally responsible for his deeds.

At verse 13 there is a break in the thought. The question arises as to guilt for sin apart from knowledge of the law. Sin was in the world from the beginning. Though the Mosaic law was given centuries later, there was law before in the reason and conscience. Sin was real because there was disobedience to the law of God in the heart. But such sin was not counted as sin in the way that it was after the Mosaic law pointed it out and forbade it. When the law was given, there was greater responsibility and hence greater guilt. The tyranny of death began with the fall and continued, though many did not sin in a specific act of disobedience after the manner of Adam's transgression.

2. *Adam and Christ* (*vv. 15–19*)

Reference to Adam opens the way for Paul to present the truth about Christ and about grace in a series of striking contrasts. Adam was "the figure of him that was to come," that is, the antitype of Christ. They are alike but infinitely different. Let us try to sum up Paul's thought in the following statements: (1) Adam is the head of mankind; so is Christ, but he is also the Head of a new humanity, the redeemed of the Lord. (2) The trespass of Adam brought condemnation and death; the righteousness of Christ brought justification and life eternal. (3) The disobedience of Adam made men sinners; the obedience of Christ has made it possible for men to become righteous. (4) Death is mandatory for all who sin; but life is voluntary, dependent on faith in Christ. (5) Men are condemned because of kinship with Adam; but they may be justified by faith in Christ.

All that Paul says is designed to impress the wondrous nature of grace and the reality of Christ's saving work. Grace is more powerful than sin. It is God's remedy for sin, the free gift of his love. Sin is a tyrant, but grace sets men free. Sin separates from God, but grace reconciles men to God. Salvation by grace, therefore, is God's response to the need of sinful men. The creative wisdom, compassionate mercy, and eternal purpose of God, all brought to focus in the sacrifice of Christ on the cross, have achieved salvation from sin.

3. Sin and Grace (vv. 20-21)

The climax of this passage is seen in verses 20-21. Paul points out the true function of the law. It points out sin and, in that sense, makes it abound. It shows the vast amount of sin, the awful sinfulness of sin. The abundance of sin serves only to show the desperate need for grace. Where sin abounds, grace abounds much more. God's grace in Christ is adequate for every sin and greater than all sin.

In verse 21 sin and grace are described as "the warring queens." How true to the history of the human race is Paul's statement: "Sin hath reigned unto death." It slays and kills. Its tyranny has filled the world with sorrow and suffering, corruption and violence, lust and blasphemy, shame and death. But sin's reign is being overthrown. The grace of God has come in to "reign through righteousness unto eternal life by Jesus Christ our Lord." Not sin, but grace, is the final word; not death, but life, is God's purpose for mankind. Not hopeless condemnation, but a way of salvation, is the glorious message of the gospel.

This is the message which the world needs so desperately to hear. It gripped the mind and heart of Paul with such conviction that he longed to preach it everywhere. He knew it to be the power of God unto salvation. Modern Christians ought to share the same burden of conviction. The stewardship of the gospel is the staggering responsibility of all who have received the grace of God. It is the supreme means by which they can help to accomplish God's plan of the ages. It is their supreme force for changing the world order for good.

The reign of sin is spreading moral chaos and spiritual doom around the earth. But grace is arrayed against sin. Grace is mighty to save. It brings hope to the despairing and eternal life to the spiritually dead. "The grace of God that bringeth salvation hath appeared to all men, teaching us that, denying ungodliness and worldly lusts, we should live soberly, righteously, and godly, in this present world" (Titus 2:11–12). This is God's answer to the plight of mankind.

5

Christian Sanctification

Romans 6:1 to 7:25

THE DOCTRINE of sanctification has been grossly misunderstood and seriously neglected. There are some groups which have made it the central teaching of the gospel. Also, they have confused sanctification with extremes of emotionalism and with claims of sinless perfection, while their behavior has often been completely out of harmony with their claims. By their extremism they have brought sanctification into disrepute in the thinking of some Christians and some non-Christians.

Much more serious, however, is the neglect of sanctification by the majority of Christians. Their ignorance of scriptural teaching has caused them to think of sanctification either as impossible of attainment or as something theological and theoretical. Many seem content to think of sanctification as a doctrine to be believed rather than a quality of living to be achieved. Their indifference arises from unwillingness to meet the demands of holy living.

But Christian sanctification cannot thus be neglected by those who want to understand the Christian gospel and who want to try to live in obedience to Christ. It relates to Christian duty. It is a part of Christian growth. It affects Christian influence. It has much to do with Christian happiness. And it ought to be foremost in Christian purpose.

A word of explanation as to the meaning of sanctification is in order. Negatively, it is not sinless perfection. Bible teaching gives no justification for any Christian to claim that he has reached a state of sinlessness or for him to hope that he will ever reach such a state during this life.

The Christian life ought to be an experience of growing victory over sin and of growing likeness to Christ, but the goal will always be ahead of us to challenge our strongest desire and effort.

Sanctification in New Testament teaching has a twofold meaning. First, every Christian is sanctified in the sense that he is set apart or dedicated to the purpose and service of God by his conversion experience. That is, he is a saint or a "holy one." Second, every Christian ought to be in the process of becoming sanctified, that is, becoming more righteous, becoming more unselfish, becoming more obedient, becoming more Christlike. It is this second aspect of sanctification which is of utmost importance for our consideration. It is the subject of Paul's teaching in the sixth and seventh chapters of his letter to the Romans.

This brings us back to Paul's illuminating treatment of gospel truth. He has completed the treatment of the first major phase of his theme—the righteousness of God which all men need and which can be received by faith in Christ. He now comes to the second phase of this theme— the righteousness of God which is to be achieved in the Christian's life through his victory over sin. Paul has dealt with the wondrous doctrine of justification. And now he turns, with the beginning of chapter 6, to the inspiring doctrine of sanctification. A Christian is obligated to demonstrate to the world the quality of his new life.

In reality, chapters 6 to 8 are a unity. They treat the new life in Christ. But the emphasis in chapters 6 and 7 centers chiefly on the conflict with sin, while chapter 8 treats more definitely the realities of the new life in the Holy Spirit. In 6 and 7 Paul answers the criticism of salvation by grace and the claims of some, as Erdman suggests, that it encourages sin (6:1–14), allows sin (6:15 to 7:6), and makes the law a sinful thing (7:7–25).[1] If we want to understand the moral and spiritual conflict raging in every Christian's life and the heavenly challenge to sanctification which our conversion experience imposes on us, we must study seriously the truth in these two chapters.

I. The Result of Regeneration—6:1–14

Spiritual regeneration is simultaneous with justification. A Christian has a new heart as well as a right standing with God. It is the new heart—a new life within—that gives promise of sanctification.

1. A Lesson from Baptism (vv. 1–4)

First of all, Paul calls attention to the objection of the Judaizer or the pagan or the person who utterly misunderstands justification by faith and salvation by grace. Such persons claim that if salvation is by grace, then grace is really an encouragement to sin, because the more one sins the more God's grace abounds. With this charge of his critics in mind, Paul asks, "Shall we continue in sin, that grace may abound?" Such is a horrible thought. Paul repudiates it as utterly illogical and as really absurd. Since we are dead to sin through the experience of grace, how can we have any desire to continue in it? The criticism that the doctrine of salvation by grace encourages sin results from complete misunderstanding of what salvation is, what grace is, what faith in Christ does to one's life. Grace does not encourage sin; it rather encourages righteousness. It is a dynamic compulsion to a new way of living, as we shall see.

Paul uses baptism to illustrate the point and to teach a very important truth about Christian experience. Baptism is a pictorial representation of spiritual regeneration. It declares personal faith in Jesus Christ, who died and was buried and rose again from the dead. Baptism represents the believer's confession of having died to sin and of having been raised up spiritually to a new life. Baptism, which is properly by immersion, is therefore a dramatic portrayal of death and resurrection. It has absolutely no meaning unless it does represent a spiritual experience of the soul. Paul seeks to remind every Christian, assuming that he has been baptized according to New Testament meaning and form and order, that his baptism has been a confession before God and men of his purpose to "walk in newness of life."

Many interpreters of these verses try to make Paul teach a sacramental concept of baptism. They claim that the relation with Christ is established through baptism, that the new life comes to the believer in the rite of baptism. In part, they base their view on the phrase "baptized into Jesus Christ." Lenski agrees with A. T. Robertson in saying that the preposition for "into" denotes sphere and not motion, even though he then becomes quite illogical and says that baptism initiates one into the Christian faith.[2] Robertson is consistent in saying, "Paul was not a sacramentarian."[3]

Paul could not be consistent and give sacramental value to the rite of baptism. He could not maintain that justification is by faith and faith alone, as he does in 3:27–31, and that we are justified by the blood of Christ, as he does in 5:8–9, and at the same time maintain that baptism is the way one comes into a saved relationship with Christ. When he says that we "were baptized into Jesus Christ" and "were baptized into his death," he means that we were baptized "in relation to Christ" and "in relation to his death." Our baptism declares our union with him in connection with his death; that is, we have faith in his atonement for sins. "We are buried with him by baptism into death," by which we declare that we have died to sin; and "as Christ was raised up from the dead by the glory of the Father," we declare by baptism that we have experienced a spiritual resurrection by the power of God. We thus pledge to walk in newness of life.

While there is nothing here to give a sacramental concept of baptism, we must be on the strictest guard against making baptism a *mere* symbol. It is symbolic, but it is symbolic of tremendous truth. If a person is properly baptized, on the basis of a real experience of conversion and with proper instruction as to the meaning of this rite, it will be a confession and commitment of such spiritual significance that the Christian's life will be influenced by it.

The lesson from baptism is as important as it is plain. It is meant to be a reminder and spiritual challenge to Christians. We have made a confession of our faith in Christ. We have declared the reality of a conversion experience, a regeneration. Therefore, we are under sacred obligation to make the Christian life true to Christian baptism. Our manner of life—words, deeds, behavior in public and in private, dealings with others, and all moral practices—is to show the reality of our relation to Christ.

2. *A Fact in Experience* (*vv. 5–11*)

As we have seen, baptism is meant to declare a fact in Christian experience. That fact is spiritual union with Christ. In conversion there has been a death to sin and an experience of new life within the heart. This is a new kind of life. It has new moral quality and new moral power. It is on this ground that Christian sanctification is the expected result of justification by faith or regeneration through the power of God's Spirit.

In all these verses the apostle emphasizes in the strongest way that the Christian is one with Christ in death and resurrection. Death and resurrection cannot really be separated. If our death to sin is real, resurrection to newness of life is also real—at least, it is normal. The old man was actually put to death that the body marked by sin should be made of no effect or put out of operation.

Paul's words mean that there is reality in the experience of regeneration. We have experienced something that causes us to hate sin. The whole moral nature has been changed at its source. If repentance is real, one has changed his mind about sin and utterly turned from it. If faith in Christ is real, he has committed himself to a new Lord. If regeneration is real, the Christian has in his inner being the living Christ. All this is a part of the reality of union with Christ which ought to issue forth in Christlike living.

A radical change takes place in conversion. It is a once-for-all experience. Christ died once, and death no longer has dominion over him. He died for sin once for all, and so his relation to sin came to an end when he gave his life for sin; and now he lives in an eternal relationship with God. The Christian has experienced the benefits of his death, which made possible redemption from sin; and now he enjoys the benefits of his resurrection in that he has the power of the living Christ to effect sanctification in his life. On this basis Paul says, "Reckon ye also yourselves to be dead indeed unto sin, but alive unto God through Jesus Christ our Lord."

We are to live in keeping with the fact of Christian experience, the fact of spiritual regeneration, the fact of union with Christ having been established by faith and being continued by faith and being fruitful for the ends of sanctification. Grace is more than absolution from sin; it is a dynamic antidote for sin. It never encourages to sin; it constrains one to hate sin and flee from it.

3. A Moral Obligation (vv. 12-14)

What Paul has said, showing that sanctification is the rightful expectation of regeneration, in no way lessens the personal responsibility and moral obligation with respect to goodness. Holiness of life is possible because one has become a Christian, but it is not an automatic result of conversion. The Christian must feel the awful weight of obligation resting on him to choose what is good, to follow after righteousness, to strive for moral excellence.

This is clearly taught by Paul's strong exhortation not to let sin reign in one's body, not to yield to the lusts of the flesh. The members of the body ought never to be given over to the works of unrighteousness resulting in sin. Instead, we must yield ourselves to God and make every capacity of the body an instrument of righteousness in keeping with his purpose. We ourselves determine the level of our sanctification. We must take God's side in the fight against sin. We must recognize our own moral responsibility. We must feel that the redemption of Christ has made every member of the body, every capacity of life, holy and sacred. We must practice self-control and must dedicate all our energies to the will of God.

We have inspiring encouragement in Paul's assurance: "Sin shall not have dominion over you: for ye are not under the law, but under grace." A Christian—a regenerated person—is no longer under the dominion of sin. Its power has been broken by the redemption of Christ. We are not, therefore, helpless victims of sinful desire within ourselves or of sinful assaults from without. We can gain a victory over sin, not because of the law forbidding it, but through the power of grace by which we have been saved.

The compulsions of grace are those of inner spiritual power and spiritual gratitude. There is inner aversion to sin, moral energy to resist sin, and constraining motivation to please the Heavenly Father. The fact that we are under grace puts in our hearts a hunger for righteousness and a desire for Christlikeness. We ought, therefore, to strive with confidence to achieve a Godlike righteousness in our own experience of Christian living.

II. THE OUTCOME OF SPIRITUAL MOTIVATION—6:15 to 7:6

We have seen that Christian sanctification has its prospect, first of all, in the initial experience of conversion. The Christian has a new heart, and therefore he is expected to live the life of a new man in Christ. The motivations for living on this level are inward and spiritual. Such is the thought Paul now develops in the next part of his letter.

1. A New Master: Illustration from Slavery (6:15–23)

Again the objection to justification by faith or salvation by grace is faced: the contention that salvation on this basis allows sin. "God forbid," says Paul. This is never the case. The very opposite is true. We are not under law, but this does not provide an excuse for sin. Law does not motivate sanctification, but grace does.

Paul now uses two illustrations, the first of which is slavery. A slave serves one master. No one can serve two masters. A person is therefore a slave of that to which he gives obedience or that which he recognizes as his master. The two masters here involved are sin and righteousness. The Christian has made his choice. Once he was the slave of sin. He acknowledged sin as master. He lived according to the ways of sin. But now he has renounced sin as master and has chosen righteousness. This is the very essence of repentance. It is a renunciation of the way of sin and a turning to the way of righteousness with such contrition of heart and earnestness of purpose that it means a genuine right-about-face. No person can choose Christ as Saviour without choosing righteousness as his goal. He thus commits himself as a slave of righteousness.

The apostle breaks out in thanksgiving: "God be thanked" for that great life-changing experience on the part of Christians. They have heard the way of salvation and learned about a new way of living. They have believed it, accepted it, and committed themselves to it. Thus they have "obeyed from the heart" the doctrine of salvation by grace and a radically new concept of morality and spiritual living. Paul is declaring that a Christian is not free to sin but set free from sin, not only in the sense that he is forgiven, but also in the sense that he has become a servant of righteousness. The motivation for Christian sanctification, therefore, is inward. The law is now written on the heart and in the mind (Heb. 10:16). Allegiance to a new master, whose ways are purity and uprightness and justice and love, becomes a constraining incentive for a new way of living.

Paul does not emphasize it at this point, but the background of his thinking is the centrality and supremacy of Jesus Christ. A Christian is not a slave of righteousness in the abstract. It is a commanding moral ideal, a divine standard, but it is much more. This righteousness is related to Christ, found in him, motivated by him, exemplified by him, and sought after in response to his lordship and in order to please him.

Paul seems almost to apologize in verse 19. Note Williams' translation: "I am speaking in familiar human terms because of the frailty of your nature." Paul understood the weakness of human nature and knew the necessity for Christians to find true freedom through voluntary submission to the ideals and practices of righteousness. He makes a vigorous appeal to Christians by reminding them of the contrast between the old life and the new. The unregenerate person yields himself to uncleanness. His moral insight is faulty. His moral inclinations are corrupt. His moral resistance is weak. The result is filthiness and lawlessness. But the new life in Christ is set in a different direction. Moral values are now understood. Moral purposes have been quickened. A Christian seeks to achieve righteousness with holiness or sanctification as his goal. "It is a life process of consecration, not an instantaneous act." [4]

In the old life, when we were servants of sin, we did not recognize the obligation to righteousness or respond to the demands for purity and truth and love. The result was a kind of conduct of which we are now ashamed. It may have included pride and unbelief, or it may have included covetousness and lying and adultery, or it may have included drunkenness and violence and profanity. For all the works of the flesh, the Christian will be genuinely ashamed. The end of all those things is death. The life in sin is a state of death now and leads to eternal death and torment forever.

What Paul is trying to help us to see is that, having been set free from sin, we have become servants of God, and the fruit or outcome of the Christian life is sanctification, "and the end everlasting life." Sin always pays off in death. The wages are always paid. It is a matter of receiving just compensation for one's deeds. But over against that, in striking contrast, God's free gift is "eternal life through Jesus Christ our Lord." This is not a matter of payment or of desert or of earning; it is a gift of divine grace. It is the priceless gift from heaven. It is a new kind of life in its source, in its power, in its quality, and in its destiny. It is a kind of life that can bear the fruits of sanctification, the fruits of the Holy Spirit—even "love, joy, peace, long-suffering, gentleness, goodness, faith, meekness, temperance" (Gal. 5:22–23).

2. A New Relation: Illustration from Marriage (7:1–6)

Paul now calls upon the analogy of marriage to emphasize the spiritual motivation for sanctification. According to the law, a woman is bound to her husband as long as he lives. If he should die, she is released from the obligation to her husband. If she were to be married to another man while her husband lives, she would of course be an adulteress. But if her husband is dead, she is free from the obligation that bound her to her husband and may be married to another man.

Christians "are become dead to the law by the body of Christ." Through his propitiation for sins Christians are set free from the law, made dead to the law, that they may "be married to another," that is, come into a new relationship with Jesus Christ as Saviour and Lord. What Paul says points back to the conversion experience of death to sin and resurrection to new life—an experience which brought new spiritual purpose and new moral power—all to the end that "we should bring forth fruit unto God."

Before this wondrous experience of salvation by grace, "we were in the flesh," we were living according to the sinful passions and desires of the unregenerate nature. These passions wrought in our bodies and brought forth results in the nature of death. The law itself "acted upon the powers of body and of mind to produce results which led only to death."[5] But when we found deliverance from the law through faith in Christ, when we died to sin by which we had been held in bondage, we came into union with Christ as Redeemer and as Lord, so that now we delight to serve him "in newness of spirit, and not in the oldness of the letter."

The motivation for sanctification is not legal requirement, but spiritual allegiance and affection. We now enjoy a freedom to do right, to do good, to obey the hunger of the heart for righteousness, to yield ourselves in glad submission to the will of Christ our Master. We are not compelled by a standard without but a compulsion within. We are joined to One who is truth and love and holiness. We love him because of his great love for us. Because we know him in the reality of redemption and in a relationship of grace and in a fellowship of wholehearted commitment, our hearts burn within us to please him and obey him and be like him.

III. THE CONTINUING CONFLICT WITH SIN—7:7–23

In the remaining part of chapter 7, Paul deals with the Christian's continuing struggle against sin in the Christian's life. As long as we live in the flesh, there will be warfare between the new nature in Christ and the old nature still resident in the flesh. Paul writes from experience. And his experience is duplicated in the life of every Christian. Sanctification must be achieved through a process, one that involves the severest sort of conflict and calls for the strongest sort of determination.

1. *The Law of God Is Good* (7:7–13)

What Paul has just said in the opening verses of this chapter gives rise to the question, "Is the law sin?" His reaction to the suggestion that the law is sin is utter horror: "God forbid." Paul goes on to show that the law of God is good, provided we understand its function to point out sin. The law is utterly impotent as a means of salvation, and it is insufficient to produce righteousness. Already Paul has said, "By the law is the knowledge of sin" (3:20); also, the law came in "that the offence might abound" (5:20). He has said that sinful passions are aroused by the law (7:5). His purpose now is to show that the law is good for its purpose but that it cannot relieve the soul suffering under the conviction of sin or be the means of effecting the righteousness which ought to characterize the life of the saved person.

Paul uses the illustration of the Tenth Commandment: "I had not known lust, except the law had said, Thou shalt not covet." The Commandment against coveting arouses the desire to covet. How true to life this is! When something is prohibited, we want it all the more. This shows something of the natural perversity of mankind, and it is true to experience after one has become a Christian. Paul says, further, that sin receives incentive from the commandment to work "all manner of concupiscence" or every kind of evil desire. When the law commands, "Thou shalt not," it seems to stir up the strongest sort of desire for violation and wrongdoing. Apart from the law, sin is dead, or seems to be in a dormant state. But let the law point it out, and then sin comes to life and springs into action.

In a further testimony out of experience, Paul refers to his former sense of false security. "I was alive without the law once." This may refer to the innocence of childhood, but more likely it refers to his feeling of self-sufficiency as a proud Pharisee before his conscience awoke to a deep sense of moral responsibility. But something happened to make the commandments of God real, and then sin revived. It became alive and made Paul conscious of his death in sin.

The commandment, therefore, which was holy and good and meant for life, became the means of death. Actually, it was not the law of God, but sin, Paul says, "taking occasion by the commandment, deceived me, and by it slew me." The law was only the tool or instrument; sin did its deceptive and deadly work. What Paul says is an exact description of Satan's work. He deceives and he slays. He never gives up in his effort to thwart and defeat Christian sanctification.

The central truth in this paragraph is emphasized again in verses 12–13. Paul pays the highest commendation to the law. The commandment is holy and just and good. The purpose of the law is to point out sin, to awaken the conscience, to make men aware of moral duty and spiritual need. It makes sin appear as sin. It shows that sin is exceedingly sinful. There is nothing wrong with the law. The wrong is in the heart, in the addiction to sin.

Let us keep clearly in mind the central purpose in what Paul says. He does not disparage the moral law as a moral guide. He does not say that the Christian is not under obligation to obey the law. He defends the law for its true function; but he declares again and again that the righteousness of God, either imputed or achieved, can never be the product of the law.

2. *The Law of Sin Is Always Present* (7:14–23)

The law of sin is always present in the life of a Christian. There is the continuing experience of temptation, a real life-and-death grapple with evil. The Christian life ought to be an experience of growing victory over sin, but let no one expect that he will not have to fight the tempter before the victory is won.

Such is Paul's personal testimony in verses 14–25. It is important to note that Paul speaks out of his own experience. And he is speaking of his experience as a Christian. Paul climbed to the highest level of devotion to Christ, but he discovered that the law of sin was always present. His experience is true to a larger or a lesser degree with every Christian.

Paul declares again that the fault is not with the law, that is, the law of God. This law is spiritual; it is the gift of God. The fault is with the law of sin, which is a part of the depravity of human nature. Paul declares, "I am carnal, sold under sin." The word translated "carnal" means made of flesh—according to Thayer, "wholly given up to the flesh, rooted in the flesh as it were." Paul declares that he is a creature of the flesh, as all men are. This does not mean that the flesh is inherently evil, but it does mean that it is "sold under sin," in captivity to sin. "Sin has gained entrance to it, has taken up its residence there, and from that base of operations has brought the whole personality into slavery."[6]

It is because of this law of sin, having its seat in the flesh, that Paul finds himself, through his own will and strength, utterly unable to achieve righteousness. In verse 15 he says,

"Indeed, I do not understand what I do, for I do not practice what I want to do, but I am always doing what I hate" (Williams). The very fact that he feels a real tension between what he knows to be right and what he actually achieves declares that the law (that is, the law of God) is good.

This struggle with sin is a struggle between the new nature redeemed by Christ and the old fleshly nature. Paul says, "It is no more I that do it, but sin that dwelleth in me." He wants to do right. He knows the new level on which the Christian ought to live. He is conscious of a compelling sense of duty and is constrained because of his affection for that which is spiritual. But the law of sin still operates in the flesh, and through his own strength he is unable to perform that which is good.

The words of Paul seem to declare nothing but failure. "The good that I would I do not: but the evil which I would not, that I do." He is thwarted at every turn because of the presence of sin. The explanation is in the fact that throughout this life the conflict goes on between the higher nature and the lower nature. The Christian finds that, when he wants to do good, evil is present: the law of sin is in operation. In the inward man, that is, on the level of the new nature, one delights in the law of God. But the law of sin works in the members of the body, warring against spiritual desire and purpose and holding life in slavery to the things of evil.

How true all this is in our experience as Christians! We aspire to holiness. If we are serious in our devotion to Christ, we strive to achieve real righteousness. We want to be mastered by the will of God. But we find, sometimes to our amazement and sometimes almost to despair, that Satan never gives up, that the law of sin operates in our members. We have ideals, but fail to achieve them. We abhor evil, but find ourselves yielding to it. Our hearts are a battlefield. The conflict is between the new self and old self. We need to understand the nature of this conflict. But God forbid that we should justify submission to evil because of it. The law of sin is always present; but there is a way to victory, and we must claim it.

IV. The Prospect for Victory—7:24–25

Paul did not despair, except that he did despair of achieving righteousness through his own strength. When he thought of the law of sin and the weakness of the flesh, he cried out, "O wretched man that I am! who shall deliver me from the body of this death?" Paul felt as though he were chained to a corpse from which he could not be delivered. But his despair immediately gave place to a declaration of certain faith and victory: "I thank God through Jesus Christ our Lord." Paul did not expect the struggle to cease. He knew that with his mind, his true purpose in union with Christ, he would serve the law of God. But he knew that he would still be subject to the weakness of the flesh. He steadfastly looked for victory not through his own strength but through the power of the Holy Spirit.

---

[1] Erdman, *op. cit.*, p. 69
[2] Lenski, *op. cit.*, pp. 391–392
[3] Robertson, *op. cit.*, p. 361
[4] *Ibid.*, p. 365
[5] Erdman, *op. cit.*, p. 77
[6] Knox, *op. cit.*, p. 501

6

Life in the Spirit

Romans 8:1-39

ALL WHO READ the Scriptures with insight agree that Romans 8 is one of the most majestic and inspiring of all the peaks of divine revelation. In this chapter Paul rises to the highest level of spiritual insight as he comes to the climax of his treatment of the doctrine of salvation. He begins with the soul-thrilling truth that there is no condemnation for the Christian and closes with the soul-strengthening truth that there is no separation from the love of God. In between he sweeps the gamut of Christian experience from the liberation of the soul in conversion to the glorification of the soul in heaven.

In order to understand and appreciate the revelation of truth in this chapter, we must see it in relation to what has preceded. It is a part of the larger section beginning with the sixth chapter. In the earlier chapters of the epistle Paul dealt with man's need of salvation, with God's provision of salvation through Christ, and with the way of salvation through faith. In chapters 6–8 we learn of the obligation of the Christian to live a new kind of life, and we discover the divine resources which make it possible to live on the level of holiness, serene faith, and certain victory. Here we see salvation in its comprehensive meaning, which includes the whole process whereby we are to be conformed to the image of the Son of God.

The means whereby this glorious prospect is to be achieved is the activity of the Holy Spirit. It is appropriate, therefore, to study this chapter under the title, "Life in the Spirit." We shall see that the life in the Spirit is one of spiritual freedom, filial obligation, blessed assurance, and eternal security.

I. Spiritual Freedom—8:1-11

There is the closest sequence between the end of the seventh chapter and the beginning of the eighth. But what a contrast! Paul has just spoken about "captivity to the law of sin." But now he declares with an outburst of thanksgiving that "the law of the Spirit of life in Christ Jesus hath made me free from the law of sin and death."

1. God's Saving Act (vv. 1-4)

A fact stated.—"There is therefore now no condemnation." Of course, this refers only to those who "are in Christ Jesus." The "therefore" points back to what Paul has been saying in his preceding argument, but particularly to the thought in chapter 7. In spite of the fact that the Christian is in a continuing struggle with the law of sin in his members, there is no verdict of condemnation against him. There is no charge, no indictment, no judgment, no penalty—because he is "in Christ Jesus." As Robertson comments, "This is Paul's Gospel."[1]

This is just another way of declaring the truth of justification by faith. Apart from Christ, one is condemned because of sin. But through faith in Christ one is pardoned. Christ died for us. We have been justified by his blood. We are no longer exposed to God's wrath against sin. We have been raised up to a new life. Hence, there is no condemnation. This freedom from condemnation means freedom from past sins and pardon for future sins.

All this emphasizes the fact of a transforming experience which gives one a new standing before God because of a new relationship with Christ. The heart can be lifted up in praise and established in peace. Because of this experience, a Christian strives no longer to walk after the flesh but after the Spirit.

The fact explained.—"For the law of the Spirit of life in Christ Jesus hath made me free from the law of sin and death." In a sense, this verse is the theme of the entire chapter. The life in the Spirit is a life of spiritual freedom. A divine power has made us free and continues to work in us. This is our hope of victory over sin. The Holy Spirit makes effective in us the resurrection power of Christ. We thus experience the moral and spiritual energy of the living Christ through his Spirit. We are no longer helpless victims of the law of sin in our members if we draw upon the resources of the indwelling Spirit. His power in us can give us the victory.

It is highly important that we understand the spiritual freedom we now enjoy. It has its source in Jesus Christ. It stems from his redemption. We have been delivered from the bondage of evil. This freedom is anchored in an experience of real conversion. Something happened through God's saving act. We were set free. We were set in a different relation to the law of sin and death, and this is prophetic of moral achievement and spiritual sanctification. Further, our spiritual freedom is inward. No outside standard could emancipate us. Faith and morality are inseparably related and are, first of all, a matter of the heart. We are free, not in our own strength, but through the power of the Spirit implementing what Christ has done for us and what Christ purposes in us.

Christ's death necessary.—The law was impotent. It "was weak through the flesh." Both the moral code and law of conscience were helpless to make us good. But God did something through the incarnation and crucifixion of Christ. He sent his own Son into the world, who was in the likeness of sinful flesh but without sin. Sin could not overcome him. He came because of the sin in human hearts. Through his vicarious death God "condemned sin in the flesh." That is, "he condemned the sin of men and the condemnation took place in the flesh of Jesus." [2] All the purposes of the incarnation converged in the death of Christ, because all the purposes of the incarnation focused upon the purpose of redemption. By Christ's death he put to death the one having the power of death, that is, Satan.

God's purpose clear.—God's saving act had a moral objective: "that the righteousness of the law might be fulfilled in us." Since we have been set free from sin, since we have experienced a moral renewal through regeneration, and since we no longer walk according to the flesh but according to the Spirit and in his power, we can achieve the requirements of the law of moral goodness. Too great stress cannot be put upon the fact that God's first objective in saving us from sin is that we may renounce sin and resist sin and resent sin. Righteousness has been bestowed upon us that the fruits of righteousness may be seen in us. We are set free from sin that we may live after the Spirit.

2. *Life on the Old Level* (*vv.* 5–8)

By way of emphasis, and to make the strongest appeal possible, Paul warns about living on the level of the flesh. Actually, he describes the contrast between life on this level and life in the Spirit. His purpose is to cultivate a strong conviction as to our duty in Christ.

Two modes of life, in all their oppositeness, are clearly shown. (1) Those who live by the standard of the flesh think constantly about fleshly satisfaction; but those who live by the standard of the Spirit are always thinking about the things which pertain to the Spirit. (2) The flesh is corrupt and weak; the Spirit is life-giving, energizing, sanctifying, always harmonious with God. (3) The mind or disposition of the flesh is death; the mind of the Spirit is life and peace. (4) The flesh is hostile toward God; the Spirit is harmonious with God. (5) Those who live according to the flesh cannot please God; those in the Spirit are a great delight to God. In other words, there are two forces at work. One is the old nature corrupted and weakened by sin; the other is the new creation indwelt by the Spirit, which produces the fruits of life and righteousness.

In the possession of spiritual freedom, we are no longer to live on the old level, no longer to walk after the flesh, no longer to be ruled by the flesh; but we are to live on a new level of purpose and power and Christlikeness.

3. The Indwelling Spirit (vv. 9-11)

As we have already observed, our spiritual freedom rests upon God's saving act and the continuous presence of the indwelling Spirit. At this point it is important that we test ourselves. If the Spirit of God dwells in us, we are no longer "in the flesh." That is, we are no longer controlled by the flesh, no longer devoted to the satisfactions of the flesh. It all depends upon whether one has the Spirit of Christ. If he does not, he is not a Christian.

If one's conversion is real, he is actually indwelt by the Holy Spirit. This means also that he is indwelt by Christ. This truth is clearly taught in verses 9-11 by Paul's use of different terms with the same meaning—"the Spirit of God," "the Spirit of Christ," "Christ," and "the Spirit." The indwelling Spirit is the assurance of eternal life. The body must die because of sin, but the spirit is alive because it has come into right standing with God. There is also the assurance of a future resurrection. The resurrection of Jesus is a guarantee of our resurrection. The Holy Spirit will also quicken our mortal bodies. The indwelling Spirit is therefore the assurance of a bodily resurrection.

Herein is the glorious climax of our spiritual freedom. First of all, it means justification and the forgiveness of sin. Secondly, it involves energy to overcome the power of sin and to live on the new level of righteousness. On this level it is possible to please God and to do the will of God. In the third place, this freedom will mean ultimate deliverance from the presence of sin in the glory of eternity.

II. FILIAL OBLIGATION—8:12-17

But let us not misunderstand our freedom. It is not freedom from obligation; it is rather the freedom of the sons of God to fulfil the implications of that relationship to the Father and to enjoy the blessed privileges of their inheritance. Nothing is more important for Christians than a profound realization, constant and inspiring, that they are the sons of God.

1. Life on the New Level (vv. 12–14)

We are confronted by the fact that "we are debtors." This grows out of all that God has done for us. We are in debt because of Christ's sacrifice for our sins, because of God's redeeming love, and because of the activity of the Holy Spirit in making spiritual freedom a reality. This freedom, however, is not to be an occasion for the indulgence of the flesh. It is meant to constrain us to rise to the new level of life according to the mind of Christ.

In verse 13 we have the key to the whole matter of Christian sanctification, the means whereby we can live the Christian life on the level of goodness. We are still subject to the temptation to "live after the flesh." This will not mean life, as many people foolishly think. It leads to death. But we can "through the Spirit" put to death the deeds of the body. The word used by Paul means "cause to be put to death." The Holy Spirit is the agent, but we ourselves must say the word that will cause him to do it. "He is the divine Executioner. But he must have our permission. . . . God does nothing in us without our own active cooperation."[3]

The whole matter of rising to this new level waits on our trusting the Holy Spirit to put to death the sinful habits and satisfactions of the lower nature. If we really want them to be put to death, he will do it effectively, and we shall enter into life which is life indeed—full, free, joyful, victorious, well pleasing to God. The proof that we are the sons of God is that we are led by the Spirit of God.

2. Trust in the Father (vv. 15–17)

These are wonderful words setting forth the relationship of Christians to the Heavenly Father. We enjoy a relationship of love and trust. Therefore, we are not in bondage to fear. Fear ought never to control the life of the sons of God. Knowing that we have received the spirit of adoption, we draw near to God and say, "Abba, Father." Why should we be afraid? We should rather act like children.

86 THE GOSPEL ACCORDING TO PAUL

Paul's phrase puts emphasis on the fact that God is our Father by using the word "Abba," the Aramaic word for father. It seems to stress the intimacy of our relationship with God. Thus we cry, "Father, Father." The Christian life takes on more and more meaning as we think of the fatherhood of God. He is near and personal. He wants the best for us. He deals with us in love, though his dealings include the severest discipline. We know that he will always do for us that which is best for us.

In this filial relationship with our Father-God, a relationship of trust and love, the Holy Spirit bears witness "that we are the children of God." The word "children" suggests something of a kinship by nature, that is, it emphasizes our regeneration. The use of "sons" in verse 14 suggests something of the legal relationship through adoption. Likely Paul had no sharp distinction in mind. The important truth is that we can have assurance through the inner witness of the Spirit that we are Christians.

As the children of God, we can be sure of our inheritance. We are the heirs of God in the sense that we partake of his nature, we have received his goodness, and we can claim his promises. We are joint heirs with Christ in the sense that we share in his kingdom. Even so, there is a condition. In order to share fully in his kingdom, we must be willing to suffer with him. We must share in the redemptive sacrifice if we expect to share in the redemptive glory. What right can we have to partake of the Saviour's crown unless we are willing to share his cross?

Let us magnify our sonship. We have been adopted into God's family. The obligations to be obedient, to exemplify the qualities of godliness, to live sacrificially, are all given the utmost meaning because God is our Heavenly Father. Our trust should lead to faithfulness, and our love should inspire sacrificial service.

III. BLESSED ASSURANCE—8:18–30

We have seen that the life in the Spirit is one of spiritual freedom and filial obligation. In verses 18–30 it is described as one of blessed assurance. The revelation of truth becomes more and more sublime. The curtain is drawn back and we get glimpses into eternity. But equally important, we discover that the Christian can live in a world of evil, can experience the sufferings of this life, and can relate himself to perplexities and hardships which are a part of human experience, all with steadfast faith and sure hope.

1. *The Hope of Glory* (*vv. 18–25*)

Paul's reference in verse 17 to suffering with Christ leads to the consideration of the right attitude toward the sufferings in this life. We can endure them with fortitude because of our hope of glory and the pledge of a completed redemption. However terrible present suffering is, it is "not worthy to be compared with the glory which shall be revealed in us." What Paul said had very real meaning for first-century Christians, and it has equal meaning for Christians of this generation.

Suffering is a normal part of Christian experience. It is a part of the earthly life. Some of it is due to the consequences of sin. Some of it is due to the sins of others; the innocent have to suffer along with the guilty. Some suffering is a part of God's disciplinary dealing with us. It is an expression of his grace and is meant for our good. Again, a great deal of suffering will be involved in redemptive service, that is, if we really bear a cross in keeping with our Christian discipleship. Paul said to the Philippians, "For unto you it is given in the behalf of Christ, not only to believe on him, but also to suffer for his sake" (1:29).

Whatever the cause of our sufferings, we can endure them when we remember the glory of the life to come. Paul is thinking about a finished redemption, of our sharing in the glory of Christ in eternity. What steadying assurance this should give to those who suffer from the ravages of disease, to those who are victims of injustice and wickedness, to persecuted saints in many places, and to all Christians who have felt the hard blows of inescapable tragedy and cruel circumstance and crushing affliction.

Paul now points out that the whole created universe has suffered from the blight of sin in human experience and in some mystic way longs for the consummation of man's redemption. The whole creation earnestly looks forward to "the manifestation of the sons of God." Paul's language is full of poetic imagery, but it sets forth a basic truth. The creation was subjected to vanity, not voluntarily, but because of the sovereign will of God. It felt the impact of man's fall into sin. It also shares in the hope of redemption.

All this emphasizes the supremacy of man in God's created universe. His fall affected the world in which he lives. But the time will come when the creation will be "delivered from the bondage of corruption into the glorious liberty of the children of God." The groaning of creation indicates something of the alarming tragedy of evil. The redemption of creation indicates something of the wonder and greatness of Christ's redemptive work.

Moreover, Paul says that we Christians, who have the first fruits of the Spirit—that is, the first instalment—have our groaning for the fulfilment of our redemption. In other words, we yearn for the fruition of our adoption in the redemption of the body. At that time, "we shall have complete redemption of both soul and body." [4]

This is indeed the hope of glory. Such hope is central in our Christian salvation. "In hope we were saved." The object of our hope has not yet been realized. But the hope of glory is still our highest hope, and because of that we wait with patience for it. There is something better yet. It is more wonderful than our finite minds can grasp, more glorious than imagination can conceive. It is a bright vision that leads us forward and imparts steadfastness and perseverance regardless of trial or disappointment or failure. Because of our hope of heaven itself, we are made strong to endure.

2. *The Help of the Spirit* (*vv. 26-27*)

Every paragraph from this matchless chapter is a new facet of brilliant truth about the life in Christ. These particular verses give us another ground for blessed assurance. The Holy Spirit is our helper—particularly, our helper in prayer. In the perplexing experiences of life, we are often baffled, bewildered, and blinded. We are often confused about duty, about affliction, and about the raging power of evil in the world order. And therefore we do not know how to pray for ourselves, for others, and for the cause of redemption. The Holy Spirit "helpeth our infirmities." That is, he helps us in our weakness. Paul uses here a graphic word for help. It means that the Spirit takes hold of our difficulty face to face at the same time, or he lends a hand to help us at the same time. Thus the Holy Spirit helps us as we pray. We do not understand the things for which we should pray. But the Spirit himself (not "itself") "maketh intercession for us with groanings which cannot be uttered." He intercedes for us with agonizing earnestness. He knows how to translate our requests into acceptable petitions before the Father because he has perfect understanding of God's will and he is in perfect harmony with God's will. The Holy Spirit thus becomes our prayer partner.

As we contemplate this marvelous picture of the Holy Spirit helping us to pray, we ought to remember that Jesus Christ ever lives to intercede for us (Heb. 7:25). He is our Advocate with the Father. And we have the Holy Spirit in us and along with us, interceding for us "according to the will of God." Thus we have two members of the Trinity helping us to pray, one with us to guide and strengthen us, the other interceding in our behalf at the throne of grace. The Christian ought to rise to the highest level of prayer, the highest level of faith, and the highest level of service.

3. *The Purpose of God* (*vv. 28–30*)

These brief verses contain treasures of truth that should fill our hearts with praise. They ought also to supply the foundation for a philosophy of life built upon steadfast faith in God. What the apostle says about God's providences and purposes constitutes the basis for unshakable assurance as to the outcome of salvation.

90 THE GOSPEL ACCORDING TO PAUL

There is certainty in what Paul says: "We know that all things work together for good to them that love God, to them who are the called according to his purpose." In spite of suffering and weakness, in spite of persecution or hardship, or in spite of anything and everything, God is in control. For those who love him and who have a sense of his call and who are committed to his purpose, he makes all things "work together for good." In other words, a gracious providence overrules all of life. That providence is the outworking of God's will for his children.

The emphasis needs to be put where Paul placed it, namely, that God is the effective cause. He can turn sickness and misfortune, hardship and persecution, sorrow and death, all of life's experiences into a means of blessing for those who keep on loving him, for those who want his purpose to be fulfilled in them. We cannot always see that all of life's experiences work out for our good. We must trust a loving God; we must walk by faith. Knowing that this word is true, we ought to be lifted above the level of worry and complaining and bitterness and fear and doubt.

God's providences are a part of his larger purpose for his children. That purpose is the consummation of his work of redemption. God's sovereign grace is the explanation of salvation from beginning to end. He chose us for salvation before the foundation of the world (Eph. 1:4). He purposed that we should be "conformed to the image of his Son," that is, that we should grow more and more into the likeness of Christ and thus more and more into the likeness of God himself. Those whom God foreordained unto eternal life, he called; those whom he called, he also justified; those whom he justified, he also glorified. Paul declares the fact of glorification as though it had already taken place. It is of course still in the future, but it is absolutely certain of fulfilment.

Here, then, we have the climax of God's redemptive work in Jesus Christ and through his Spirit. His purpose is that the sons of God shall be like the Son of God. His sovereign purpose and power are the guarantee of future glorification. The God of grace is the God of purpose, and the God of purpose is the God of power. Through his living Spirit the grace freely bestowed upon lost men has its fulfilment in their regeneration and in their coming to resemble his own likeness and to share in his glory. "Behold, what manner of love the Father hath bestowed upon us, that we should be called the sons of God: ... Beloved, now are we the sons of God, and it doth not yet appear what we shall be: but we know that, when he shall appear, we shall be like him; for we shall see him as he is" (1 John 3:1–2).

IV. ETERNAL SECURITY—8:31–39

This passage is the capstone of Paul's marvelous exposition of the righteousness of God. To understand and appreciate it as we should, we need to review Paul's argument up to this point. He has shown the awful guilt of man because of the universality of sin and because of God's wrath against sin. He has set forth the wondrous truth about justification by faith and the way of salvation by grace. He has interpreted the truth about sanctification and portrayed the new life in Christ. Now he comes to the climax of his argument in a burst of exultant assurance that nothing can defeat the purpose of God's grace, because nothing can separate the believer from the love of God in Jesus Christ our Lord. On this basis, we have eternal security.

What Paul has written in these verses ought to answer every question one can raise about the ultimate outcome of faith in Christ. But there is more in this passage than the divine affirmation of spiritual security. There is also a challenge to Christians to demonstrate to the world the faith, courage, and joy which ought to result from the conviction that there is no separation from the love of God.

1. God Is for Us (vv. 31–32)

Paul begins with a question, as he so often did. "What shall we then say to these things?" What "things" did he have in mind? Perhaps his mind turned back to all that he had been saying about God's salvation and God's sovereign purpose of grace for his children. But likely his thought pointed more definitely to "the sufferings of this present time," to the temptations and trials of life, to the infirmities and hardships which are common to experience. What can Christians say, what assurance can they have, in the light of life's perplexities and perils? Paul gives three answers. The first one is, God is for us or God is on our side.

The question, "If God be for us, who can be against us?" is rhetorical. It did not imply doubt. Paul put it that way for emphasis. Since God is for us, it makes no difference who is against us. We need no greater security. God believes in us. He is friendly toward us.

We really have overwhelming evidence that God is for us. He spared not his own Son but gave him up for us all. No one can comprehend what went on in the heart of God when he delivered up Christ to death in our behalf. God saw our need, our guilt in sin, our helplessness to save ourselves, our utter ruin because of sin. In response to this need and because of his grace, God went to the length of giving his own Son to be the propitiation for our sins. If God was willing to go this far, "how shall he not with him also freely give us all things?" Specifically, he will give us the full benefit of his redemption to guarantee for us an abundant entrance into his everlasting kingdom.

In the light of what God has done, we can have no question that his attitude toward us is one of redemptive longing, infinite love, and compassionate mercy. The resources of God have been expended to the point of the cross of Christ. Therefore, we can be sure that God's investment in our salvation will not come short of fruition.

2. There Is No Charge Against Us (vv. 33–34)

Again Paul asks a question: "Who shall lay any thing to the charge of God's elect?" In other words, who can make any indictment against the Christian? No indictment can stand because God is the one who justifies. The Christian has been justified by faith. He has received forgiveness for sin. He is a trophy of divine grace and has a standing before God which no one can alter. Since our sins are against God, and he has justified us freely "by his grace through the redemption that is in Christ Jesus," there can be no one to bring a charge against us.

We have the same idea repeated in the question, "Who is he that condemneth?" There was condemnation for sin. We deserved the wrath of God. But Christ died in our behalf. Through him we have received the atonement. He was made sin for us that we might be made righteousness.

The apostle goes on to declare the great central facts of Christ's redemptive work. He died, he arose from the dead, he ascended to the right hand of God, and he makes intercession for us as our great High Priest. Through his death he became the curse for us. Through his resurrection he proved the validity of his sacrifice and the reality of his power over sin and death. His ascension reveals his majesty and declares his sovereign power. As our Advocate, he pleads the merits of his sacrifice for all our sins, past, present, and future. Because he ever lives to intercede, he is able to save unto the uttermost.

3. *Nothing Can Separate Us from the Love of God* (*vv. 35–39*)

Once again, for argument and emphasis, Paul asks a question: "Who shall separate us from the love of Christ?" In verse 39 we have "the love of God." The love of Christ and the love of God are the same in meaning. Paul calls the list of the severest trials: tribulation, distress, persecution, famine, nakedness, peril, and sword. The apostle knew in his own experience the reality of these trials. Christians through the centuries have been called on to endure them. They do not separate us from Christ's love. They may separate us from wealth and health, from family and friends, from comfort and ease. But they can have absolutely no effect upon the unchangeable love of God.

It is to be admitted that such hard experiences seem to do us great injury. Quoting from Psalm 44:22, Paul says that these trials are like an experience of slow torture. It seems that we are being "killed all the day long," that we are "accounted as sheep for the slaughter"—all for God's sake. But such suffering does not mean that God's love has changed or that anything has separated us from it. Instead, all these trials give opportunity for God's love in Christ to demonstrate its power. In all these things we can be "more than conquerors through him that loved us." Paul is saying that we can keep on living victoriously. We can be conquerors with a margin! We can do it through Christ, whose love never fails.

Now we come to Paul's triumphant affirmation of faith. With inspired understanding and deepest emotion he traverses the entire range of experience and existence to declare that nothing can separate us from God's love in Christ. Nothing in experience—"neither death, nor life"; nothing in the hierarchy of invisible powers, either good or evil—"nor angels, nor principalities, nor powers"; nothing in time or space—"nor things present, nor things to come, nor height, nor depth"; nothing in all creation—"nor any other creature." Nothing shall ever "be able to separate us from the love of God, which is in Christ Jesus our Lord."

We thus learn the wonder and the glory of God's love in Christ. It is unchangeable and infinite; it is constant and sufficient; it is eternal and triumphant. God loves us no matter what is happening to us. His love is as dependable as the North Star—indeed, far more dependable, as dependable as the eternal Sun of Righteousness, the same yesterday, today, and forever!

Such is the life in the Spirit, the new life in Christ, the life of righteousness by faith.

---

[1] Robertson, *op. cit.*, p. 372
[2] *Ibid.*
[3] Ralph A. Herring, *God Being My Helper* (Nashville: Broadman Press, 1955), p. 25
[4] Robertson, *op. cit.*, p. 376

7

God's Purpose in History

Romans 9:1 to 11:36

ANYTHING following the triumphant affirmation at the end of the eighth chapter of Romans seems to be an anticlimax. We have been lifted up into the heavenlies of spiritual security, and our hearts rejoice in our eternal salvation. But let us remind ourselves that our Christian faith calls for much more than rejoicing in our own wonderful salvation. Our experience with Christ ought to impart to us a deep concern about God's purpose in history. It is in order, therefore, to come to the study of chapters 9–11, which pertain to this matter.

These three chapters have to do primarily with the unbelief of Israel and God's rejection of the chosen nation. How is this related to the outcome of God's promise to Israel? How is it related to God's plan of the ages? This is the problem which Paul treats in this section of his letter. It was natural for Paul to face the problem about Israel's unbelief, and it was highly important for him to set forth for his readers in Rome his understanding of God's redemptive activity in history.

I. GOD IS SOVEREIGN—9:1–29

Here is a fact, an eternal truth. God controls the universe, and he rules in the affairs of men. His authority and power are absolute. His sovereignty, therefore, is the first truth to consider in connection with his purpose in history, and his saving work of both Jews and Gentiles must be seen in the light of this truth.

1. Paul's Burden for Israel (vv. 1-5)

Paul could not think of the eternal security of believers without thinking of the eternal condemnation of unbelievers. Therefore, his whole being reached out with concern for the lost, and especially for the Jews, his kinsmen according to the flesh.

In these verses he expresses his grief and unceasing pain because of the tragedy of Israel. So acute is his concern that he uses a threefold oath: "I say the truth in Christ, I lie not, my conscience also bearing me witness in the Holy Spirit." This was appropriate since he was known personally to few of the Christians in Rome. He could almost wish himself "accursed from Christ" for the sake of the Jews. While opinion varies as to the meaning of Paul's expression—due to the form of the word for "I could wish" and the word for "accursed"—it surely indicates his unmeasured concern, almost to the point of wishing himself "delivered up to God for destruction" for his own brethren in the flesh.

The unusual privileges bestowed on the Israelites made Paul feel all the more strongly the tragedy of their unbelief. He mentions nine distinctive privileges: (1) They are "Israelites"—they are bearers of an honored name; they are God's chosen people; they are the people of the covenant. (2) Theirs is "the adoption"—in a special way God adopted them for his own; of Israel God said, "I loved him, and called my son out of Egypt" (Hos. 11:1). (3) Theirs is "the glory"—the presence of God with Israel was shown in the Shekinah Glory in the tabernacle. (4) Theirs are "the covenants"—God had renewed his covenant with the Israelites again and again. (5) Theirs is "the law"—this refers to the law given at Sinai. (6) Theirs is "the service of God"—this refers to the Temple services and instructions for worship. (7) Theirs are "the promises"—God had made countless promises to Israel, the supreme one being the promise of the Messiah. (8) Theirs are "the fathers" —they can claim a heritage from the patriarchs: Abraham,

Isaac, and Jacob. (9) The supreme honor of all, "of whom as concerning the flesh Christ came"—the promised Messiah had come, and he was a Jew.

Paul could not stop when he spoke of Christ as a Jew in his humanity; he had to go on and say, "who is over all, God blessed for ever." This is one of Paul's clearest declarations of the absolute deity of Christ. It is true that the last part of verse 5 is the center of much argument as to whether Paul does in this verse identify Christ as God. It depends largely on the proper punctuation. The original Greek text had no punctuation. But the punctuation of the King James Version is in every way natural. In fact, other punctuation makes an awkward construction. The most convincing factor, however, is the logic of Paul's thought. In contrast with his statement about Christ in his human nature, Paul would naturally affirm his divine nature. The deity of Christ is not dependent on this one verse, but we understand this verse to declare that Christ is very God.

2. *God's Promise According to Election* (*vv. 6–13*)

The first five verses of the chapter are introductory to the problem Paul faces: Has the promise of God to Israel failed? Paul answers that question clearly in verses 6–13 by showing that the promise is according to election. First, let it be noted, "they are not all Israel, which are of Israel." Not all the seed of Abraham are the true children of Abraham. God determined that Isaac would be the heir of Abraham and the heir of the promise made to Abraham. Thus, the promise of God was according to choice or according to election. Note, also, that the birth of Isaac was the fulfilment of a special promise to Abraham.

The apostle adds a second example that God's promise is according to election. After Rebekah conceived, but before Esau and Jacob were born, God decreed that the older should serve the younger; he chose Jacob rather than Esau to be the heir of promise.

The truth emphasized by the apostle is that the promise made to Israel was an expression of God's own sovereignty.

In his choice of Jacob, nothing either good or evil on the part of Jacob or Esau determined God's choice. His choice was an act of pure grace "that the purpose of God according to election" might depend wholly upon himself.

3. *God's Dealings Not Unjust* (vv. 14–21)

Is God to be accused of unrighteousness or injustice? Paul answers, "God forbid"—perish the thought! God never deals with men in arbitrary fashion. He is always just. Even so, God is the Creator, Sustainer, and Ruler of all things and all men, so that he has a right to deal with men according to his will. Paul calls attention to God's word to Moses, "I will have mercy on whom I will have mercy, and I will have compassion on whom I will have compassion" (see Ex. 33:19). Moses learned that a part of God's goodness is his sovereign mercy. It is in no sense dependent on human will or effort. God dealt with the children of Israel in mercy; he cannot be accused of injustice.

Another illustration is found in Pharaoh. The divine purpose in raising up Pharaoh was intended for good to all mankind: "That I might show my power in thee, and that my name might be declared throughout all the earth." God "displayed this power in the interest of Israel so that Israel might see with what a mighty hand he was fulfilling for them the old promises which had been made to the patriarchs . . . This is not mere omnipotence or omnipotence set over against mercy but omnipotence serving mercy." [1] God had a larger purpose in mind in his dealings with Pharaoh, but in no sense was God unjust to Pharaoh, for he did not harden Pharaoh's heart until Pharaoh had repeatedly hardened his own heart.

To find fault with God for acting in this fashion or to question the morality of his actions is utterly incongruous. God is the potter, and man is the clay. How foolish for a vessel to say to the potter who formed it, "Why hast thou made me thus?" The potter has power over the clay to do with it as he pleases, to make one lump a vessel unto honor and another unto dishonor. Likewise, God acts within his right to do as he pleases in his dealings with men, for he is their Creator and their Keeper. All that God did with Israel must be interpreted and evaluated in the light of God's sovereignty and righteousness.

4. *God's Mercy Shown* (*vv. 22–29*)

God can never be rightly accused of treating men unjustly. His mercy was repeatedly shown in the life of Israel and also in his dealings with the Gentiles. As an evidence of this, he "endured with much longsuffering the vessels of wrath fitted to destruction" or ready for destruction. His sovereignty "is never exercised in condemning men who ought to be saved, but rather it has resulted in the salvation of men who deserved to be lost."[2] Paul relates this both to Jews and to Gentiles.

To emphasize this further, Paul refers to two Old Testament prophets, Hosea and Isaiah. He quotes the word of God through Hosea, "I will call them my people, which were not my people; and her beloved, which was not beloved." This doubtless refers to the wayward people of the Northern Kingdom of Israel. So wayward did they become that God sent judgment upon the nation in the captivity of the ten tribes. They became scattered throughout the Gentile world. But God will yet show mercy and claim some for himself. Through God's mercy they will yet "be called the children of the living God."

The quotation from Isaiah also emphasizes God's mercy. Likely it refers to the wayward people of Judah in the time of Isaiah. God declared that "a remnant shall be saved." In another quotation from Isaiah, Paul emphasizes that the mercy of God is the sole explanation of preserving a seed or a remnant. Otherwise, the destruction of the Jews would have been as Sodom and Gomorrah.

The apostle stresses the truth that the sovereignty of God is not without mercy. His long-suffering patience with the chosen people proved his willingness to save and confirmed the fact that Israel's failure was not the fault of God.

II. Man Is Responsible—9:30 to 10:31

God's sovereignty is absolute, but man's will is free. With our finite minds it is impossible to harmonize God's absolute sovereignty and man's freedom. Both are facts. We do not have to harmonize them. We can humbly accept them. And we must accept them if we want to understand God's purpose and God's activity in history.

1. Israel's Rejection Due to Unbelief (9:30 to 10:4)

Already we have learned that the promise to Israel was according to election, but we have learned also that it was conditioned on faith. Since salvation is conditioned on faith, the unbelieving person is responsible for his lost condition.

Paul faces the fact that many Gentiles have attained to the righteousness of faith, while the Jews generally had not attained to the righteousness of faith. This seems to be a paradox. The Gentiles were not seeking after righteousness, that is, in their paganism they were not constrained by moral ideals and purposes. On the other hand, the Jews followed after the law of righteousness and sought to attain righteousness on that basis. The difference was that the Gentiles responded to the gospel with faith, while the Jews responded to it with unbelief. Christ became for them a stumbling stone and rock of offense. They were rejected because they rejected the Christ of God. Through the centuries Christ has been for those who reject him the rock of destruction but for those who accept him the rock of eternal salvation.

Paul feels an unceasing agony of concern for the salvation of Israel: "Brethren, my heart's desire and prayer to God for Israel is, that they might be saved." He has never ceased to do his utmost to win the Jews to Christ. He knows their guilt. He feels the weight of their condemnation. He longs and prays that they might know the saving power of the gospel. But Paul understands their difficulty. They are zealous for God, but in the wrong way. Through wilful ignorance, through pride in their own righteousness, and through rebellious unbelief toward Christ, they have been unwilling to submit to God's way of salvation and receive his righteousness by faith.

All such efforts were futile. Had the Jews been willing to understand, they would have learned that "Christ is the end of the law for righteousness to every one that believeth." Christ fulfilled the law, and he was the goal of the law; but the meaning of verse 4 is that "Christ ended the law as a method of salvation . . . Christ wrote *finis* on law as a means of grace." [3] After Christ came, the law could no longer claim control of anyone whether Jew or Gentile. The logical conclusion is that the rejection of Israel was the fault of Israel.

2. Salvation Offered to All on the Same Terms (10:5–13)

This passage is one of the clearest in the Scriptures on the way of personal salvation. It teaches not only the responsibility of the individual, but it affirms with much emphasis the inward and spiritual nature of salvation and the universal nature of the gospel.

The Jews made the tragic mistake of trying to earn righteousness by the law. Moses described that kind of righteousness and said that "the man which doeth those things shall live by them." If righteousness could be by the law, perfect obedience would be necessary. But the Jews had never been able to keep it. They boasted about the law but dishonored God by breaking it (2:23). No other one has been able to meet the requirements of the law in his own strength: "There is none righteous, no, not one" (3:10). God's way of salvation is righteousness by faith.

This righteousness, Paul says, does not demand human merit or effort. No one needs to ascend into heaven to bring Christ down, and no one needs to descend into the abyss to bring Christ up from the dead. Instead, the message of the gospel is right at hand—in the mouth and in the heart. Everyone has direct access to the Saviour. Salvation is available to men not by law but by faith, not by sacrament but by grace. That was the gospel which Paul preached.

Confession and faith naturally go together. Paul is not talking about a false faith but a genuine faith. Salvation depends on the right response to Christ, which of course must include believing in his divine nature and actual resurrection and receiving him as the one sent of God to save men from sin. This is what faith means. And confession by the mouth is the natural declaration of the belief in the heart. The confession confirms an experience which is already complete, a decision already reached, an attitude already felt. Belief with the heart must be voluntary, not forced; it must have love and devotion. Confession must be voluntary and genuine; it declares acceptance and commitment.

In verses 11–13 Paul declares again that the gospel is in every sense universal. In the first place, it meets universal needs. There is no distinction between men in the sight of God, whatever the nation or race or class. All men have sinned, and all men apart from Christ are lost. In the next place, the gospel is the revelation of universal love and universal sovereignty, for the Lord is over all and is infinitely rich in mercy toward all men. Finally, the gospel is universal in its invitation and offer: "Whosoever shall call upon the name of the Lord shall be saved." Jews and Gentiles are invited on the same terms. Whoever will call with contrition and sincerity and humility and trust—God will hear and forgive and save.

3. *Responsibility of Christians* (10:14–15)

It is impossible to know just how these verses relate to what precedes and what follows. Some of the commentators think that the connection is with what precedes, and so they feel that Paul is emphasizing the unbelief of the Jews, who refused to hear the message preached to them. God had sent messengers with the good news. Thus it is claimed that "the reason for Israel's alienation lies in herself." [4]

We cannot feel that the viewpoint just stated is correct. It seems rather that the apostle was caught up, as he stated the universal elements of the gospel, with an overwhelming realization of the responsibility of Christians to proclaim the gospel to all men. At any rate, verses 14–15 do set forth with gripping force truths which Christians should take to heart with utmost seriousness. God's purpose in history is a clarion call to every Christian to accept the role of a missionary. That is, he should feel the obligation to declare the good news of the gospel and to entreat lost men to be reconciled to God through faith in Christ. The lost cannot be saved without believing. They cannot believe without hearing. They cannot hear apart from messengers of the gospel. And messengers cannot go to the uttermost part of the earth unless they be sent.

Here is the desperate urgency for missions. The message of salvation, which is meant for all mankind, fails of its purpose if those who have received it betray the genius of their faith and fail to share it with others.

4. *Good Tidings Rejected* (10:16–21)

Now Paul resumes his treatment of the responsibility of the Jews. They had indeed heard the gospel message—not all, but great numbers. It had been widely preached, but the Jews had not hearkened to it. The prophetic word of Isaiah, "Lord, who hath believed our report?" was descriptive of the perversity of the Jews in their unwillingness to hearken to the message of salvation. With dramatic emphasis, Paul asks, "Have they not heard?" In reply he quotes from the psalmist to imply that the gospel had been preached throughout the Roman world.

He quotes also from Moses to show that God dealt with the heathen in a way to provoke Israel to jealousy and anger. A similar thing was happening in Paul's day in that the conversion of the Gentiles was meant to be a means of challenging the Jews to an acceptance of the gospel. Israel cannot excuse herself for lack of knowledge. Isaiah had declared the same truth, speaking for God, "I was found of them that sought me not; I was made manifest unto them that asked not after me." God's word through the law and his word through the prophets should have made Israel responsive to the gospel. Spiritual opportunity came, but it was rejected. God's compassion was shown through his persistent and long-suffering entreaties.

What sin is so black as wilful rejection of God's entreaties and the riches of his grace in Christ? What tragedy is so terrible as the judgment of God on those who refuse his saving mercy?

III. God's Purpose Will Be Fulfilled—11:1-36

We need the long look with respect to God's saving work in Christ. And we need to keep in mind the sovereignty of God, the power of the gospel, and the mighty activity of the Holy Spirit, all of which give us assurance that God's purpose in history will be fulfilled.

1. A Remnant Has Been Saved (vv. 1-10)

Paul faces the question frankly, "Hath God cast away his people?" Can it be that those to whom the promise was made have been utterly repudiated? "God forbid." Paul himself was a Jew, a member of the chosen race, and a member of the honored tribe of Benjamin. But he was a Christian. It could not be that God had completely and finally rejected the Jews. And Paul was not alone. Many of the Christians at Rome were Jews. A much larger number of Jews in other parts of the Empire had accepted the gospel. Therefore, at least a remnant of Israel had already been saved.

The same truth is illustrated by Paul by reference to the Old Testament. When Elijah cried out in despair on Mount Horeb that the prophets of God had been killed and that he alone was left, God answered, "I have reserved to myself seven thousand men, who have not bowed the knee to the image of Baal." Paul declares, "Even so then at this present time also there is a remnant according to the election of grace." Some Jews have believed, but their salvation is the result of the election of grace. It is not due to the works of the law or righteousness of their own or to their racial inheritance. It is due solely to God's grace.

Paul's conclusion is clearly stated by another reference to Israel's history. Israel as a nation failed to achieve the righteousness sought after, but it was because of unbelief. What the nation as a whole failed to achieve, a remnant by the election of grace did achieve. "The rest were hardened." Stubborn unbelief brought the judgment of God upon them. Old Testament prophets predicted, "God hath given them the spirit of slumber, eyes that they should not see, and ears that they should not hear." This condition continued to prevail after the gospel was preached. The punitive hardening of God was severe because, in fulfilment of a prediction in the Psalms, the Jews let their law and their advantages become a snare and trap and stumbling block. God rejected Israel as a whole, but he saved a remnant.

It is not impossible to win Jews to faith in Jesus Christ. No group of people is to be given up as beyond the reach of the gospel. The fact that God has saved a remnant by the election of grace is certain proof of a larger purpose, not only for the salvation of the Jews, but for the salvation of all races and nations.

2. The Gentiles Are Being Saved (vv. 11-24)

Paul now shows that the unbelief of Israel has opened the door of opportunity for the Gentiles, and thus God's purpose in history is being accomplished. Therefore, God has overruled Jewish unbelief and made it a means of glory to himself and blessing to the world.

This truth is brought out clearly in verses 11-12. Thinking backward of God's judgment on Israel because of unbelief, Paul raises a question, "Have they stumbled that they should fall?" His answer is his customary "God forbid" or perish the thought. The attitude of the Jews in rejecting the gospel led more quickly to preaching the gospel to the Gentiles.

Another aspect of God's purpose is "to provoke them to jealousy." By seeing the Gentiles turn to Christ, the Jews may be moved to jealous desire to receive the blessing of salvation. Often jealousy leads to hardening and more stubborn rebellion. But, contrariwise, it often leads to a repentant spirit. The salvation of the Gentiles can, therefore, be divinely blessed for the salvation of the Jews. Paul expands the thought by suggesting in verse 12 that if the fall of Israel has resulted in the riches of the world and the failure of Israel the riches of the Gentiles, how much more will the salvation of the Jews already converted and yet to be converted turn out to the fulfilment of God's redemptive purpose for all, regardless of race or nation.

Paul is writing chiefly to Gentiles in Rome. Therefore, he impresses upon them his zeal in preaching to the Gentiles, hoping that their conversion may provoke the Jews to emulation. He would do everything in his power for the salvation of those of his own race. The rejection of the Jews had already meant the reconciling of the Gentile world. He believes firmly in their future conversion, and this will be like a resurrection from the dead. Israel was a holy nation, set apart for God's purpose. The first fruit of that nation was the patriarchs of old. They were the root of the tree. The branches also are holy. "But this does not mean that the fact of belonging to Israel is itself enough to shield anyone from God's wrath, . . . Branches of the holy tree may become useless and be cut off; and that is what has now happened to a large part of the people of Israel." [5]

In verses 17–24 we have the illustration of the olive tree, which further interprets God's purpose in history through the salvation of the Gentiles. Paul declares that many of the branches have been broken off. That is, many of the Jews have been rejected because of unbelief. In their place many Gentiles had been grafted. They were like the branches of wild olive. Therefore, the Gentiles are warned against pride over the Jews. They are not the root but the branches. Their opportunity to be grafted in has come because the natural branches were broken off, and this because of unbelief. The Gentiles have their place by faith. They have no occasion to be high-minded. Rather, they should consider with reverential fear the goodness and the severity of God. The goodness of God has come to them, and the severity of God has come to the Jews. How humble and grateful the Gentiles ought to be. How hopeful the Jews ought to be, "for God is able to graft them in again."

3. *Israel Will Yet Be Saved* (*vv. 25–32*)

This passage is of great importance. It points to the ultimate outcome of God's redemptive purpose in history and, particularly, to the salvation of the Jews. What does Paul mean by saying that all Israel will be saved? How is this related to "the fulness of the Gentiles"? The views of scholars vary. We shall be wise to avoid dogmatic interpretation, but we can be certain as to the central truth set forth by the apostle.

The importance of this problem is indicated by Paul's concern that the Roman brethren should not be ignorant of this mystery. This "mystery" is not something mysterious, but a truth formerly hidden which is now made known. God's will had been revealed to Paul in a special way, especially his purpose of redemption for all men. The Gentiles in Rome need to understand that the hardening which happened to Israel is not final. It is temporary, "until the fulness of the Gentiles be come in," that is, until the gospel is made known to the Gentiles and God's purpose in their salvation is accomplished. We should not stress the completion of one before the beginning of the other. The conversion of the Gentiles will yet stir up the Jews to a realization of their opportunity, "and so all Israel shall be saved."

What are the scope and meaning of this prediction? It cannot mean that Jews who have died without faith will be saved. It cannot mean that at some future time every living Gentile will be saved and every living Jew will be saved. Christ declared that the wicked and the righteous will live together on the earth until his return. It cannot mean that all Jews will be saved en masse, because salvation is an individual matter. It cannot mean that all Jews will be saved just because they are Jews, because God is no respecter of persons. It cannot mean that all Israel, meaning all Israelites, will be saved; the true Israel is the spiritual Israel.

But Paul's words do mean, in the judgment of this writer, that there will be a mighty turning on the part of the Jews to the Lord. The stubborn unbelief of the chosen people will give place to faith. The persistent effort of the Jews to "establish their own righteousness," not according to God's way, will give place to penitent and trustful acceptance of the righteousness of faith. Thus, "all Israel," not the nation as a unit, not the race as a favorite of God, but the true Israel, the spiritual Israel, the Israel of faith, shall be saved. They will acknowledge him whom Isaiah foretold, the Deliverer out of Zion, Jesus the Messiah, who will turn ungodliness from Jacob through the fulfilment of his covenant and the blessing of his forgiveness.

It must be pointed out that Paul is understood by many people to be foretelling Christ's return at the end of the age and the almost universal salvation of the Jews following his return. Our views about the millenium may vary; but there is no room for doubt that God's purpose in the salvation of the Jews will be fulfilled.

Paul reminds the Gentile believers in Rome that the Jews have been counted enemies of the gospel for the sake of the Gentiles, but as touching the election of grace they are beloved for the sake of the patriarchs with whom God made the covenant promise. He will yet fulfil it. The present unbelief of the Jews has been used and is being used of God for the salvation of the Gentiles. God's purpose is, also, that the mercy being shown to the Gentiles will yet open the way for the Jews to obtain mercy. All have been shut up, Jews and Gentiles, in unbelief, that he might have mercy upon all, both Jews and Gentiles. There is no distinction between the Jew and the Gentile. God yearns to save all, and offers his grace to all.

4. God Is His Own Interpreter (vv. 33–36)

There could be but one response as Paul contemplated God's sovereignty, God's purpose in Israel, and God's redemptive activity in history: His soul burst forth in a sublime doxology of adoring praise: "O the depth of the riches both of the wisdom and knowledge of God!" Paul had scaled the heights of spiritual vision as he thought of God's saving work in Christ, of his elective grace, and of his hope of glory in the redemption of men.

Paul declares that there are realities in the mind and heart of God utterly beyond human comprehension. We cannot understand his judgments or decisions. We cannot trace out his ways. No one can fathom the infinite mind of the Lord. No human being can be his counselor. No one can merit his favor. He is the source, he is the way, he is the goal. All things are of him and through him and for him. To him be glory forever!

Paul's doxology has the utmost meaning as we relate it to the truth which precedes. God is the clue to history. God is himself the explanation of redemption. His justice needs no vindication. His election of grace is the expression of his own sovereignty. His salvation declares his mercy.

God is his own interpreter. God is God, the God and Father of our Lord Jesus Christ, the God of salvation, the God of all men. That is enough. He is giving himself through the redemption of his Son and the activity of his Spirit and the power of his gospel to save a lost world.

Because of God's purpose in history, we can have hope and certainty. Because God's plan of the ages is a redemptive undertaking, we ought to give our utmost to the cause of world evangelization.

---

[1] Lenski, *op. cit.*, p. 614
[2] Erdman, *op. cit.*, p. 109
[3] Robertson, *op. cit.*, p. 388
[4] Nygren, *op. cit.*, p. 385
[5] *Ibid.*, p. 398

8

Righteousness in Christian Living

Romans 12:1 to 15:13

NOTHING is more important for Christians than a deepening conviction that the righteousness they have received by faith is to be demonstrated in daily living. The unanswerable testimony as to the reality of Christian experience is a Christlike life.

With the beginning of chapter 12 there is a transition in Paul's thought from the doctrinal to the practical, or from an exposition of gospel truth pertaining to inner faith and experience to an exposition of gospel truth related to character and behavior. We learn now that the new life in Christ ought to find expression through self-dedication and moral insight, through the right attitude toward oneself and toward others, through Christian citizenship and Christian love, through moral integrity and purity, and through consideration for others and strict regard for one's Christian influence.

This part of Paul's letter is an essential part of his gospel. It is as much a part of the gospel revelation as that which has to do with repentance and faith, or with election and providence. The fruits of repentance are works of righteousness. The proof of faith is a new kind of conduct. The purpose of election is that we might be holy and without blemish in the sight of God. The providences of God are meant to help us grow more like the image of his Son. Paul builds a broad and deep foundation for Christian belief. Then he calls upon us to build on that foundation a magnificent structure of Christian living. "Christian ethics emerges from Christian theology." [1] We may well think of this section, 12:1 to 15:13, as the gospel of everyday religion for personal conduct and social relations.

I. THE CALL TO FULL DEDICATION—12:1-2

This call to full dedication rests upon all that precedes and relates to all that follows. Nowhere in the Scriptures is there a more comprehensive and inspiring appeal for complete self-giving to the will of God. It ought to move Christians to an unreserved surrender to Christ for holy living and faithful service.

1. *The Constraining Motive (v. 1a)*

We have another one of Paul's convincing "therefores." It points back to the revelation of truth in the first eleven chapters. It rests upon all the wondrous realities of the grace of God in justification and of the power of the Spirit in sanctification. Paul beseeches the Christians in view of what the Christian life is: a right standing with God, union with Christ in his death and resurrection, a new life in the Spirit, and eternal security in the love of God.

Paul beseeches his fellow Christians on the basis of "the mercies of God." This is the constraining motive for full dedication. His mercies are indeed more than can be numbered. But, chiefly, Paul is thinking of God's compassions shown in all that he has done for us through Christ for our salvation. Christ died for us that we might live. Through his redemption God's love has flooded our hearts. We have spiritual freedom and Christian hope. What further incentive or more compelling motive could we have for giving ourselves to God? It ought to be observed that self-dedication is never forced; it must always be a voluntary response to God's love in Christ.

2. *A Living Sacrifice (v. 1b)*

The dedication of self must be all-inclusive. We are to present our bodies "a living sacrifice." They are to be presented as an offering, that is, given. Already Paul had made something of a similar appeal: "Yield yourselves unto God, as those that are alive from the dead, and your members as instruments of righteousness unto God" (6:13). The body stands for the totality of one's being—body, mind, and spirit. It includes all of life's faculties and capacities. But unlike the Old Testament sacrifice, which was a slain offering, the Christian presents himself "living" on the altar of service.

The body is indeed "holy." That is, it belongs to God. It should therefore be offered to God, set apart for his purpose and his alone. Along with this, there is of course the call to holiness. If our bodies are devoted entirely to God, they cannot be devoted to sin. God will not accept an offering marred by lust, covetousness, hatred, hypocrisy, or dissipation. But if our bodies are clean and strong, self-disciplined and well trained, they will be well pleasing to God.

A truth implied by "a living sacrifice" is that we are to offer our bodies as a medium of service in the kingdom of God, serving with such utter abandon that one's body is consumed in the expenditure of talent and strength for the cause of Christ. Such self-dedication is our "reasonable service." But the true meaning of this expression is "spiritual worship." When we give ourselves in holiness and service, our dedication becomes an act of worship.

3. *The New Pattern* (*v. 2*)

"Be not conformed to this world: but be ye transformed by the renewing of your mind." There is a world of difference! The negative admonition is, "stop being fashioned" or "do not have the habit of being fashioned" by the present world. Do not accept the pattern of this age. Terrific pressure will be exerted to make us do so. "This world" stands here for that sphere of life which is contrary to God. Its standards are false and sinful. Its god is the devil (2 Cor. 4:4). It is dominated by Satan. We may apply this admonition to speech, business practices, personal habits, recreation, attitudes toward other persons, and attitudes toward money. There is great danger in adopting the customs and standards of this wicked world. The Christian is not of this world; he is a citizen of the kingdom of God.

Paul's positive appeal is, "be ye transformed by the renewing of your mind." This means the mind indwelt by Christ, the mind strengthened by the Holy Spirit, the mind which is committed to the ideas and ideals of the kingdom of God. Moral transformation depends upon moral insight which comes through the indwelling Spirit and through moral purpose energized by the Holy Spirit. If we have "the mind of the Spirit," we can indeed rise to a high level of purity, unselfishness, and faithfulness.

The purpose of this spiritual transformation is that we may test and find out the will of God, all to the end of course that we may do the will of God. It is the supreme good, the thing well pleasing to God, and the perfect or complete goal of life. By living in keeping with this appeal, we test and confirm the will of God. We find that it works. It brings the greatest degree of personal satisfaction and the greatest degree of spiritual achievement.

II. Humility and Faithfulness—12:3–8

On the basis of full dedication to God, which we have just considered, Paul now makes an appeal for the translation of the ideals of goodness into one's personal life. First of all, the Christian life ought to be marked by humility. A Christian needs to have the right attitude toward himself. This does not mean self-depreciation or a mock humility. It means that we guard against exalting ourselves and magnifying our virtues and abilities. How difficult this is! Our natural tendency is to pride. We ought to have a sane view of ourselves, recognizing especially that God has blessed each person with capacities and gifts. We have no reason to exalt ourselves above others, but we have every reason to appreciate what God has done for us.

Paul clearly has in mind the fellowship of Christians in the church and the proper attitude toward self and toward others. The church is the body of Christ. Like the physical body, with many members, each one having a different function, so the church is a body, made up of many members, all closely related, all constituting a unity in Christ, but each one having unique functions and individual responsibilities. It is of utmost importance that Christians shall cultivate humility. This is among the noblest of Christian virtues. It is absolutely imperative if the fellowship of a church is to be genuinely Christian.

In the church there is diversity of gifts, each Christian having gifts according to the purpose of God's grace; and there is an obligation to use these gifts faithfully. If one has the gift of prophecy, the power to understand and proclaim the will of God, he should exercise it not in self-confidence but in faith and with fidelity to the Spirit. One may have a gift of ministering to people, another the gift of teaching, and another the gift of exhorting or comforting. Let them devote themselves faithfully to these gifts.

Another Christian may have money to give. Let him give liberally. Let the one in a position of leadership be diligent in his office. Let the one who can show mercy to the sick and poor do so with brightness and good cheer. Whatever gift one has, he faces the responsibility to use it for the glory of God and the benefit of men. The gifts from God are not meant to gain praise but to give blessing.

III. Love the Ruling Principle—12:9–21

These verses show that love is to be a guiding principle in the Christian life. Many duties are mentioned, but love is the note running through all the exhortations.

1. Love Among Christians (vv. 9–13)

(1) We are to love "without dissimulation" or "without hypocrisy." Pretended love is despicable, but sincere love is a powerful force for good will between Christians.

(2) We are to seek after goodness. Something in the soul of the Christian should cause him to abhor the evil and cleave to the good. There should be affinity for everything good but antipathy for everything evil.

(3) We are to cultivate brotherly love. The love among the members of God's family should be warm and tender and affectionate. Such love is a proof of discipleship.

(4) We are to show deference to others. With respect to any honor or special opportunity, it is noble on the part of a Christian not to seek it for himself but to prefer that a fellow Christian receive it instead. Love generates an unselfish spirit.

(5) We are to be zealous in service. Slothfulness, laziness, and halfheartedness are unworthy. Surely the service of Christ ought to be characterized by concentration of purpose, enthusiasm of spirit, and utter self-abandon.

(6) We ought to be hopeful and steadfast. Regardless of the situation in which a Christian finds himself, he can rejoice in hope. Such hope will inspire endurance in tribulation and steadfastness in prayer. Many Christians have glorified the experience of tribulation through the joy of hope and the prayer of faith.

(7) We are to practice generosity and hospitality. This means that we should distribute to the needs of the saints and show hospitality toward fellow Christians and even strangers in the name of Christ.

All these matters were important in Paul's day, and they are equally important now. Christians ought to make love dominant in their relationships with one another.

2. *Love for One's Enemies* (*vv. 14–21*)

Paul now relates the ruling principle of love to the Christian's relationships with those outside the Christian group, even enemies. Of course, there are instances when malice and violence break out among Christians. Obviously, Christian love is the only way to resolve friction and restore fellowship in such cases. The cases described in these verses, however, emphasize love for those who are set against us or those outside the Christian community.

(1) We are to forgive wrongs and insults. "Bless them which persecute you: bless, and curse not." One must have a forgiving spirit springing from real love in order to do

this. But we must do so if we are to be Christlike, if we are to avoid misunderstanding and malice, and if we are to overcome persecution in the way that Christ did.

(2) We are to share the joys and sorrows of others. It is much easier to weep with those who weep than to rejoice with those who rejoice. Christians ought to share with others in both fortune and misfortune. Thus we demonstrate unselfish interest and reveal the spirit of Christ.

(3) We must guard against selfish ambition and pride. A Christian ought to avoid selfishness in thinking about others and in relationships with others. Instead of being high-minded, he should be friendly toward those who are lowly. Always we need to guard against conceit so that we may see the good in others and see the weakness in ourselves. It takes this sort of spirit to get along harmoniously with people.

(4) Never pay back evil. Often the Christian receives evil treatment at the hands of the world, but he is not to pay back in kind. To return evil for evil will only add fuel to the flame of bad feeling. It will increase friction and provoke violence. It is far better to be imposed on than pay back evil in return.

(5) Do the honorable thing. A Christian must strive to do the appropriate, the seemly, the right thing. Such conduct will dispel many occasions for a quarrel.

(6) Strive to be at peace with others. Note that Paul says, "If it be possible, . . . live peaceably with all men." There are times when all efforts toward peace fail, but a real desire for peace is a mighty safeguard against violence. As far as possible we are to avoid an issue which would lead to a clash.

(7) Leave vengeance to God. Christians can never properly avenge themselves. They are too subject to weakness and guilt. Only God can execute that which is just. Let us avoid wrath, or keep wrath under control, and trust God to take care of our interests.

(8) Overcome evil with good. This is not mere idealism; it is the mightiest and the most practical way to overcome

evil. Kind replies can conquer bitter criticism. Love can conquer hate. By kindness "thou shalt heap coals of fire on his head." Let us remember that God is conquering sin with grace.

IV. THE CHRISTIAN AS A CITIZEN—13:1-7

The Christian must live his life as a member of society. He is a citizen of the state. Therefore, he cannot properly escape the duties of Christian citizenship. In fact, one cannot be a good Christian and not be a good citizen. Paul's teaching at this point is of the highest importance. The principle of the separation of church and state is a priceless heritage in our nation's life. But it needs to be matched with another principle: The Christian is a citizen and has a God-given obligation to translate Christian principles into civic responsibilities.

1. Respect for Civil Authority (vv. 1-5)

When Paul wrote the passage we are studying, the Roman government was pagan and completely totalitarian. It was not easy for Christians to relate themselves constructively to such a government, but it was necessary to do so. The apostle laid down basic principles which guide Christians with respect to civil authority at any time or under any political system.

"The powers that be are ordained of God." This does not mean that God approves a corrupt government, ungodly officials, or unjust legislation. It does mean that civil authority is divinely instituted and is meant to serve good ends. Therefore, it is right for a Christian to be "subject unto the higher powers," that is, to respect civil authority and be subject to it. Resisting such authority is resisting God and will lead to "damnation" or punishment by the ruler. Paul stresses the fact that the function of civil authority is the maintenance of order and uprightness: "Rulers are not a terror to good works, but to the evil." The function of government is to curb lawlessness, immorality, and the wickedness which is destructive to the welfare of the people generally. Also, it is to be "the minister of God to thee for good." Its function is to encourage all that is socially beneficial.

A law-observing person has no occasion to fear the state, but the person who defies authority and transgresses the bounds of right and freedom makes himself liable to punishment by the state. We are to be obedient to law not through fear of punishment, but "for conscience sake." The motive is loyalty to what is right in the sight of God.

It has to be admitted that in many cases civil authority comes far short of its divine function. It does not truly reflect the ordinance of God. Legislation may sanction evil practice, and law enforcement may be controlled by bribery, partisanship, or brutal injustice. But the principle enunciated by Paul still stands. Civil authority in its fundamental nature is designed of God to preserve order and justice, to encourage good and prevent evil.

2. *Support for Established Government* (*vv. 6–7*)

The Christian has duties as a citizen. Paul mentions particularly the obligation to pay taxes. This is a moral obligation. The administrators and operators of government render an aid to society generally. "They are God's ministers" and have a right to support for their services.

We therefore have an obligation to "render . . . to all their dues: tribute to whom tribute is due; custom to whom custom; fear to whom fear; honour to whom honour." Unfortunately, many public officials are not personally honorable. But the position they fill merits the respect of Christian citizens.

The teaching of Paul should be applied to all aspects of civic responsibility. Christian citizens have an obligation to vote, to offer themselves for public office, to serve on juries, to champion civic righteousness, to work for public morality, to work sacrificially for the public welfare, to contend for civil liberties, and to fight for the public defense. Christians ought to become a mighty force for morality in government, for justice and freedom for all men, irrespective of race or class, and for principles which guarantee an enduring democracy.

V. Love and Social Duty—13:8-10

The Christian moves in a wider circle of social contacts still. There is one all-inclusive principle to govern his relationships with society: "Love one another." Love is the one debt which the Christian owes all men. This debt should not be denied or regretted; it should be acknowledged and cultivated. Let no one misunderstand what love is. It is not sentimental emotion or admiration of ugly traits in some other person. It is rather active good will reaching out toward other persons with appreciation of their worth, respect for their personality, and a desire to help them. Thus, love is to relate us properly to people of other races, other nations, other classes, our enemies, all people everywhere. If we do not love men for Christ's sake, we have no kinship with Christ.

Paul goes on to explain that love will lead to the fulfilment of every social duty: love fulfils the law. The apostle quotes five of the Ten Commandments, the five most fundamental in human relations. A person who loves, according to the true standard, could never commit adultery, or steal, or kill, or bear false witness, or covet. In fact, any other commandment would be comprehended in the all-inclusive one to love one's neighbor as oneself.

VI. Christian Morality—13:11-14

This brief passage sets forth the moral imperative in Christian living. The apostle emphasizes the demand for serious devotion to a high standard of moral conduct. He really sounds out a ringing challenge to moral warfare.

1. *Spiritual Alertness* (*v. 11*)

Paul shared with the early Christians a keen sense of expectancy with reference to the return of Christ. That expectancy constitutes the background for this stirring admonition having to do with Christian morality. C. H. Dodd says that "Paul appeals to the sense of Crisis as a motive to ethical seriousness."[2] This is what the apostle means by saying, "And this, knowing the season, that already it is time for you to awake from sleep, for now our salvation is nearer than when we believed." The consummation of our salvation is nearer than when we first became Christians. Paul sought always to burden Christians with a sense of eternal values.

Christian morality calls for moral alertness. There is every reason for Christians to wake up to the reality of moral values and to realize that the issues of eternity converge on everyday moral choices and duties. It is high time to awake: it may be much later than we think. To be asleep implies forgetfulness of God, but to be awake implies spiritual readiness. A worldwide moral crisis of the gravest sort at the present time gives to this admonition of Paul the greatest meaning.

2. *Moral Action* (*v. 12*)

We are to cast off the works of darkness and put on the armor of light. "The works of darkness" refer to the works of evil, all that stands for the reign of Satan. "The armour of light" means the weapons of goodness and truth, all that is represented by the rule of Christ, really the whole armor of God. Christian morality can never be achieved apart from moral action arising from moral decision and moral commitment.

The expressions of Paul, putting off and putting on, emphasize personal responsibility. The Christian must act for himself as he puts the works of darkness utterly away and as he decisively puts on the armor of light. There is no place for compromise or indecision. And let it be observed that moral action calls for more than stern resistance to evil within one's own life: it calls for daring assaults upon all the strongholds of iniquity and the forces of wickedness which spread moral corruption in a community or which imperil the moral structure of a nation's life.

3. Moral Behavior (*v. 13*)

Williams' translation makes the meaning of this verse obvious: "Let us live becomingly for people who are in the light of day, not in carousing and drunkenness, nor in sexual immorality and licentiousness, nor in quarreling and jealousy." There must be a renunciation of the sins of flesh and spirit: the sins of intemperance and lust and the sins of jealousy and faction. There is no substitute for purity in the area of sex, for abstinence from intoxicating beverages of all kinds, for self-control that leads to moral decency and strength, and for unselfishness which makes jealousy and strife impossible. The most convincing witness Christians can give is the example of behavior according to the New Testament pattern.

4. Moral Achievement (*v. 14*)

The way to a high level of moral achievement is stated by Paul: "Put ye on the Lord Jesus Christ." The way to crowd the bad out of life is to fill life with the good. To put on the Lord Jesus Christ means to receive him into the heart, to accept his moral standards, and to depend upon his grace and strength. But along with this, we must stop making provision for the flesh to satisfy its evil desires. Apart from Christ, moral victory is impossible. In fellowship with Christ, moral excellence becomes a supreme desire and a certain achievement.

VII. CONSIDERATION FOR THE WEAK—14:1 to 15:13

Paul's concept of Christian living included concern for the weak. In this passage he dealt with how to treat fellow Christians whose faith was weak or immature, especially those with conscientious scruples about eating meats and observing special days. Obviously, this matter had become a problem in the church at Rome, as it had previously in Corinth. The instruction of the apostle gives us guidance for many choices we must make in matters of Christian relations and moral duty.

1. Respect Conscientious Scruples (14:1–12)

A group in the church, evidently a minority, felt that it was wrong to eat meat and felt that the sabbath (seventh) day was superior to other days. It seems certain that the drinking of wine was also involved (v. 21). The persons most disturbed about this matter were not necessarily Jews. Paul describes them as "weak in the faith." That is, their faith lacked full knowledge. They made superficial distinctions about personal practices. Also, they failed to understand the faith or the teaching of the gospel. To avoid eating meat that may have been offered to idols, they became vegetarians. Some few of them, likely not a large number, also held on to the observance of the sabbath. The majority of the Christians felt no such scruples of conscience. The problem arose because the overly scrupulous criticized the more liberal group and vice versa.

Let us summarize Paul's teaching about this problem as follows:

(1) He admonishes the church to receive "him that is weak in the faith," not for disputing and efforts to convince him that he is wrong, but with respect for his scruples.

(2) He urges both groups to refrain from judging the other. They are to respect the sincerity and freedom of those of opposite conviction and practice.

(3) He insists that matters of conscience are to be settled in relationship to God. God alone has the prerogative of judging. Jesus also said, "Judge not, that ye be not judged" (Matt. 7:1). The Christian must decide right and wrong on the basis of his personal accountability to God.

(4) Paul said, "Let every man be fully persuaded in his own mind." That does not mean that a Christian has a right to do as he pleases or that he is his own standard of right and wrong. But it means that he must be convinced in his own mind, irrespective of the scruples of others and without reflecting on them.

(5) The apostle declares that every person is answerable to Christ. Whatever one does he must do it with

regard to the Lord—whether keeping a day or eating meat—always giving thanks for God's gifts. No one lives to himself, and no one dies to himself. The Christian belongs to the Lord. "Whether we live therefore, or die, we are the Lord's." We have no right to judge others. "We shall all stand before the judgment seat of Christ." We will acknowledge him as Lord and give account of ourselves to God.

2. *Watch Your Influence* (*14:13–23*)

Now the apostle warns against the exercise of one's freedom in a way to do damage to a weaker brother. A person is always responsible for his influence. Many moral choices have to be settled on this basis. Some course of action may not be inherently wrong, but if it will do injury to someone else, it becomes wrong because of its bearing on others. Paul's teaching may be summed up in three admonitions:

(1) Do not exercise freedom to the hurt of others. It is nothing less than sin to put a stumbling block in another person's way. We remember the word of Jesus that it is better to have a millstone hanged around one's neck and to be drowned in the sea than to "offend one of these little ones which believe in me" (Matt. 18:6). The question is not to be decided, as Paul said, on the basis that meat is clean or not clean—that is, whether it has been offered to an idol or not. Nothing is unclean by itself. Some choices in and of themselves are neither right nor wrong. Then the question needs to be decided, as Paul insisted, on the basis of one's influence on others. If someone who lacks insight for moral evaluation will be hurt, then there is wrong involved in offending his conscience.

"Destroy not him with thy meat, for whom Christ died." This means that the moral welfare of a fellow Christian or any fellow man must be considered with respect to every course of action, every personal habit. A Christian cannot escape responsibility for his influence. The abuse of freedom will cause others to misunderstand it, to speak evil about it, and to be gravely injured by it.

(2) Understand the kingdom of God and put its values first. The kingdom is not a matter of rules and regulations, not a legal system prohibiting meat or approving vegetables, not something external or ceremonial. It is a matter of inner righteousness and peace and joy in the Holy Spirit. This instruction of Paul, however, gives no license for excessive eating or indulgence in strong drink or yielding to the flesh at any point. It rather requires real righteousness. It demands loyalty to principles of living that lead to personal uprightness and to moral influence of the highest and strongest quality. We must be mindful of the impact of our lives on others and follow the practices which make for peace. It is nothing short of sin if a Christian's influence fails to contribute to harmony or fails to contribute to the moral strength and spiritual growth of others.

(3) Practice self-denial in behalf of others. For the sake of meat, "destroy not the work of God." It would be better to give up meat forever than to hinder God's work of grace in another person's life. Paul states a principle which will guide a Christian in all matters pertaining to his influence: "It is good neither to eat flesh, nor to drink wine, nor any thing whereby thy brother stumbleth." Wine is specifically pointed out, which shows that it was a problem in New Testament times as it is now. Intoxicating drink of any kind, even with moderation, can never be justified, because it has a damning influence on others—not to speak of what it does to the person who drinks it.

Let the Christian who has mature faith never flaunt it before others and insist that he can do so and so without moral injury to himself. Let one practice self-denial rather than wreck some other person's character. Personal liberty should be secondary to the spiritual welfare of others.

Paul adds a word in verse 23 to help the person with doubt about courses of right or wrong. He is thinking, of course, about a person with scruples about matters not wrong in and of themselves. If there is doubt, let one refrain. To go against the conscience enlightened by faith is sin.

3. Imitate Christ (15:1-7)

This passage continues the emphasis in the preceding chapter but holds up Christ as the perfect example. He did not insist on his own rights; he considered the needs of others. Christians should imitate him in this particular respect, as in all others. Those who are morally strong "ought to bear the infirmities of the weak," that is, help those whose faith is weak, help those with conscientious scruples, help all who are morally defective, and help those struggling with besetting temptations. Our purpose should be not to please ourselves but to help our neighbors, to help everyone who needs our assistance. This will call for bearing the reproaches of others, just as it did in the case of Christ.

The Scriptures themselves help us at this point. Paul declared that they were written for our instruction that through endurance and encouragement we might have hope. Paul adds a prayer that the God of endurance and encouragement would grant to Christians unity of spirit that they might glorify God. Always keeping the example of Christ before us, we are to receive one another with mutual confidence and mutual concern.

4. Magnify Spiritual Unity (15:8-12)

As Paul comes to the conclusion of his treatment of righteousness in Christian living, he makes an appeal for a spiritual unity that transcends differences in the Christian fellowship. He is thinking particularly of the Jews and Gentiles. Christ had come to confirm the promises made to the Jews, but he had come also for the salvation of the Gentiles. The quotations given by Paul from the Old Testament emphasize repeatedly that God's purpose of grace includes the Gentiles, so that in the divine plan there is no longer Jew and Gentile: all are one in Christ Jesus.

Let the truth be impressed upon us that righteousness in Christian living rises to its highest level when it expresses itself in Christian love for all persons everywhere.

5. *A Benediction* (15:13)

Paul has completed his magnificent challenge to translate the righteousness of God into one's daily life—into all personal attitudes, all social relations, all moral practices, and all life purposes. He closes with a benediction, praying that God's full purpose of salvation may be realized in each Christian and in the Christian community: "Now the God of hope fill you with all joy and peace in believing, that ye may abound in hope, through the power of the Holy Spirit." Righteousness springs from faith in Christ. It can be achieved through the power of the Holy Spirit. It will make one's life rich with joy and peace and hope.

---

[1] Dodd, *op. cit.*, p. 188
[2] *Ibid.*, p. 209

9

Ambassador for Christ

Romans 15:14 to 16:27

THE LETTER to the Romans comes to a conclusion with a stirring declaration of missionary objective. In this last section we learn of Paul's burden for the extension of the gospel to the farthest limits of the Roman Empire. We feel something of his passion as an ambassador for Christ to preach the gospel to those who had never heard the good news of salvation. If we are sensitive to the impressions of the Holy Spirit, we will have a deepened conviction that world missions is the supreme mission of every church and every Christian.

With Paul's conversion there came the missionary call. The chief purpose of his life from that time forward was to witness to the gospel of the grace of God. He had a realistic understanding of the ruin of lost men under God's wrath against sin, and also an overmastering compulsion to share with them the unsearchable riches of Christ that they might be saved. It was his missionary vision and concern that constituted the immediate occasion for writing his letter to the Romans. He wanted to go to Rome; he wanted to preach the gospel there. And then he wanted to go on to Spain as an ambassador for Christ. It was his hope to enlist the support of the believers in Rome for this mission.

This last section of the letter needs to be seen, therefore, as more than a conclusion, treating personal matters and plans. It needs to be studied in the light of Paul's greeting at the beginning, 1:8–15, and in the light of his total gospel message. It may well be considered a ringing challenge to modern Christians for missionary conquest.

I. Personal Testimony—15:14–33

It was customary in Paul's time for a letter to conclude with personal matters and salutations. Paul naturally closed his letter in that way. But for him, with consuming missionary interest, it was inevitable that he should relate personal expressions to plans and efforts for the evangelization of the Gentiles. That is exactly what we have in this passage.

1. Sense of Stewardship (vv. 14–17)

Spiritual commendation, if deserved, is always in order. It helps to create an atmosphere of understanding and good will. Paul wisely commended the Christians in Rome, somewhat as in 1:8, and thus sought to cultivate on their part a favorable attitude toward his contemplated visit. He was anxious that their reaction to his letter would prepare them to receive him cordially. Their goodness and knowledge and ability to admonish one another made his letter seem almost unnecessary. This was a tactful compliment.

But the apostle was bold to remind the Christians in Rome of the grace which had been given to him or the stewardship committed to him as the "minister of Jesus Christ to the Gentiles." Paul had a divine commission. In fulfilling it, he ministered the gospel of God. His expression here declares his concept of his lifework, mainly, to serve as a priest "that the offering up of the Gentiles might be acceptable" to God. Of course, this would be realized through the sanctification of the Holy Spirit. The only hope of our service being acceptable to God is the activity of the Spirit in purifying our motives and making fruitful our efforts.

Paul had justifiable reason to glory in what had already been accomplished in the conversion of the Gentiles. But he did not take the glory to himself; he did it only "through Jesus Christ in those things which pertain to God." What the Lord had wrought through him was a part of his credentials for a new venture of faith in fulfilling the stewardship committed to him and in taking the gospel to Spain.

2. Ambition to Preach Christ (vv. 18–21)

One supreme purpose dominated the life of the apostle Paul, namely, to preach Christ and to evangelize lost men. Moreover, it was his ambition to preach Christ in virgin territory, to go into new fields, and to proclaim the good news of salvation where it had not yet been known. The missionary passion burned in Paul's heart.

The power of the Holy Spirit had been with Paul in mighty signs and wonders to confirm his witness to the gospel. In the chief cities of Asia Minor and Macedonia and Greece, he had established churches and laid the foundations for the expansion of Christianity. The moral and social life of these cities had felt the impact of the new faith. With a vision of the world field and a noble ambition to extend the frontiers of the gospel, Paul had preached "from Jerusalem, and round about unto Illyricum." The territory identified by this last phrase is not definite, but it suggests the area to the northwest of Macedonia. Thus Paul's witness had sounded out from Arabia to Illyricum. To the limit of his strength he had "preached the gospel of Christ" or fulfilled the mission committed to him.

Paul's ambition to preach "not where Christ was named" lest he should build on another's foundation was not vainglory; it was the true spirit of the pioneer, the concern of a true missionary, anxious that others and still others and yet still others would hear the message of redemption and experience the power of the gospel. One of the dangers in modern Christianity is the loss of the pioneering spirit. Too many Christians, including preachers, have worshiped at the altar of comfort and security: many have lost the spirit of daring that leads to conquest of new fields and starts Christian churches in centers where Satan has had his throne. The world is still waiting—thousands of communities in our nation, vast areas of life on the personal and social levels, and uncounted millions in the nations overseas—still waiting for the gospel which is the power of God unto salvation.

3. Plans to Go to Rome (vv. 22-29)

At the beginning of his letter (1:10-15), Paul states his longing to go to the Imperial City. Here he reaffirms his purpose and outlines his plan. So far, hindrances have prevented his carrying out his long-cherished dream. But now he feels that his immediate task in Greece and Macedonia and Asia Minor has been completed. This does not mean that these areas have been completely evangelized. It means, rather, that Christianity is firmly established and Paul can press on into new territory. It may suggest also Paul's feeling that he is not as acceptable to some of the groups as he had formerly been, so that it is wise to go elsewhere. But the heart of the matter is that Paul is bent on a visit to Rome and then a campaign in Spain.

At this point Paul tactfully expresses the hope of receiving assistance from the Christians in Rome for the next phase of this missionary work. This is part of the reason for his writing, that they might come to know him and understand his view of the gospel. Paul never begged for help. He worked with his own hands to support himself and others. But he challenged the Christians to sense their stewardship for the support of the servants of the gospel.

But first of all Paul must go to Jerusalem. He is going, along with others appointed by the churches, to take the offering contributed by the Gentile Christians in Macedonia and Achaia for the poor saints at Jerusalem. The raising of this offering had resulted from Paul's aggressive leadership in stirring up the more prosperous Gentile churches to share with the poorer brethren in Judea. It was entirely fitting that the Gentiles should share material gifts with the Jewish saints because they "have been made partakers of their spiritual things." The gospel came to the Gentiles from the Jews; therefore, they are their debtors. Paul declares that when this mission is accomplished, he will come to Rome and then go on to Spain. He looks to the future and the consummation of his plans by counting on the fulness of the blessing of Christ.

4. Request for Prayer (vv. 30–33)

These verses point out the deep concern Paul felt about his visit to Jerusalem. He entreated the Roman Christians to join with him in prayer for a successful outcome of his mission. More was involved than the deliverance of the offering. He was going with a high sense of duty and with earnest hope that he could effect genuine reconciliation between the Jewish and Gentile segments of the Christian movement. The cause of Christ would be definitely set forward by a united witness to the truth of the gospel declaring the freedom of all men in Christ, the way of salvation by grace through faith, and the objectives of the gospel in terms of Christian love and moral transformation. Paul was indeed returning to Jerusalem as an ambassador for Christ.

He was not unaware of the personal danger involved. He knew the violent hate of the non-Christian Jews in Judea. Long years before they had purposed his death. Therefore, Paul besought the Roman Christians to pray with him that the outcome of his visit to Jerusalem would mean progress for the gospel through a gracious response on the part of the Jewish saints in accepting the offering and through his own deliverance from those bent on his destruction.

In all these plans, the apostle recognizes that success must come by the will of God. His prayer is that God will prosper him in his undertaking, so that he may come to Rome with joy through God's goodness and leading and may receive the refreshment of fellowship and achievement with the saints there.

To complete his request, Paul adds a benediction: "Now the God of peace be with you all. Amen." It seems as though Paul thought of closing his letter at this point. But another chapter will be added. This inspiring benediction matches the greeting in 1:7 and expresses the apostle's sincere wish and spiritual concern for his fellow believers in Rome.

II. Fellow Workers—16:1-16

In spite of the argument of some Bible scholars to the contrary, we believe there is convincing evidence that chapter 16 was an integral part of Paul's letter. The question arises chiefly from the long list of persons mentioned in this chapter. How would Paul have known them? There is no reason why he should not have known personally many of the Christians in Rome. He had not been to Rome, but it would have been quite natural for him to have had intimate contacts with many believers there. Paul had had a prolonged ministry in both Corinth and Ephesus and shorter periods of service in other places. This would have put him in touch with a great host of persons who later settled in the capital.

1. Commendation of Phoebe (vv. 1-2)

It seems certain that Phoebe was the bearer of the letter. What could be more fitting than that Paul should introduce her with a word of commendation. She was a servant of the church at Cenchrea, the port of Corinth. The word used for "servant" is the same as that translated "deacon" in Philippians 1:1. It suggests that already churches were turning to godly women to serve as deaconesses. If it does not mean this, it at least declares that in a significant way Phoebe had served the church at Cenchrea.

Paul's appeal to the Christians in Rome was to receive Phoebe appropriately and give her assistance in her mission, whatever it was. He could vouch for her as one who had "been a succourer of many, and of myself." She was thus a Christian woman known for her helpfulness to others, and especially missionaries.

2. Salutation to Christian Friends (vv. 3-16)

Paul was interested in people. He was drawn to many by strong ties of friendship and by even stronger bonds of fellowship in serving the cause of Christ. While the apostle refrained from extensive salutations to individuals in the churches where he had served, he thought that he could single out these individuals in Rome and send personal greetings to them without being misunderstood. A brief word of commendation or appreciation identifies most of the persons mentioned.

Most notable of all are Priscilla and Aquila. They are friends of long standing, who had literally risked their lives or "laid down their own necks" for Paul. They came originally from Italy. The apostle had stayed with them in Corinth. Later they had gone to Ephesus. Now they were back in Rome. And a segment of the church in Rome meets in their house.

Epaenetus is well beloved; he was the first convert in the province of Asia (not "Achaia," according to the best texts). Mary had proved her devotion through tireless labor. Andronicus and Junias were converts to Christ before Paul. They were well known among the apostles and had at sometime shared the hardships of the gospel with Paul, perhaps imprisonment. Ampliatus was bound to Paul by special ties and affection. Urbanus had been a helper in Christ, and Stachys was a dear friend. Apelles had proved his faith in some test.

Paul remembered the household of Aristobulus, Herodion a kinsman, and the household of Narcissus, particularly those who were Christians. Tryphaena and Tryphosa, probably sisters and perhaps twins, were commended for labor in the Lord.[1] Persis was beloved by the church because she had labored much in the Lord. Rufus—who perhaps was a son of Simon the Cyrenian—stood out for some distinguished service; and Paul included his mother in the greeting because of her care of the apostle on some occasion.

Asyncritus, Phlegon, Hermes, Patrobas, Hermas, and the brethren with them were called by name; also Philologus, Julia, Nereus, his sister, Olympas, and all the saints with them. Something in their lives and service had bound them to the heart of Paul in a special way. Then Paul concluded,

"Salute one another with an holy kiss"—the common form of salutation—by which love and accord were expressed. In this closing salutation, the apostle included all the members of the church. He then added, "The churches of Christ salute you."

Paul's long list indicates sensitive recognition of his dependence upon fellow workers and of the pre-eminent place of men and women in carrying forward the work of the kingdom of God.

III. False Teachers—16:17–20

Again and again Paul found it necessary to warn the churches against selfish-minded men, sometimes arrogant and sometimes ignorant and sometimes malicious, who constituted a hindrance to the Lord's work. They caused divisions and proclaimed false doctrines that led both Christians and non-Christians astray. It was proper for Paul to admonish the Christians in Rome to be on the alert lest such false teachers should do damage to their fellowship and their witness for Christ. Perhaps some of the Judaizers were at work in Rome. But it seems more likely that the false teachers referred to here preached license as a part of liberty. Their god was their appetite. By their speech, which sounded smooth and good, but which was deceitful and seductive, they beguiled the innocent. Their teaching was a deathtrap for those not anchored in the faith.

Paul felt a genuine concern for the well-being of his fellow believers. He was glad for the obedience and devotion of the Christians in Rome but could not refrain from a word of warning in behalf of their spiritual welfare. He could assure them of the ever-present help of God to overcome Satan and, even more, of the certain final victory over Satan.

IV. Paul's Companions—16:21–24

These verses constitute a sort of postscript in which Paul includes the greetings of his companions in Corinth.

Timothy had been enlisted on the second missionary tour and had proved to be one of his most dependable helpers. He was a true fellow worker of Paul. Later on he will be in Rome with Paul. Lucius and Jason and Sosipater were kinsmen. Tertius was Paul's scribe, who wrote the epistle, and he inserts his own greeting. Gaius, Paul's host, evidently a man of means as the host of the whole church, sent his salutation; also, Erastus, the treasurer of the city of Corinth, and Quartus, about whom we know nothing other than that he was a brother in Christ. It should be noted that verse 24 does not appear in the best manuscripts.

V. Doxology—16:25-27

Paul closed his letter with a doxology of lofty expression. The power and purpose of God are the key ideas. It magnifies the preaching of Jesus Christ. It declares the plan of the ages, the revelation of the mystery, the purpose of God which reaches back to eternity before the world began and reaches forward to eternity after the world ends. That purpose was once hidden, but now it has been made known by the writings of the prophets. According to the commandment of the eternal God, the gospel is to be preached to all nations for the purpose of winning all men everywhere "to obedience inspired by faith" (Williams).

"To God only wise, through Jesus Christ, be glory for ever. Amen." The eternal God is the source of all wisdom and the essence of all glory and the end of all praise. He has revealed himself through Jesus Christ for the salvation of men. Let adoration and thanksgiving, service and love, be given to him forever!

VI. The Unfinished Mission

The conclusion of Paul's letter to the Romans looks forward to the commencement of a new missionary adventure and the continuation of a strategic missionary objective. This last section confronts us with the unfinished mission of the churches of Christ. Paul wanted to preach in Rome, so that from the very capital of the Empire the influence of the gospel might go out to the whole world with power to change the lives of men and bring them to acknowledge Jesus Christ as Saviour and Lord. He wanted to go on to Spain, representative of all the lands still waiting for the revelation of the true God and the message of eternal salvation. The apostle wanted his own life to be a living sacrifice on the altar of Christian world missions.

In the providence of God, Paul's letter to the Romans has become God's message to us. It is an exposition of the doctrines of salvation, which throb with missionary compassion, which plead with missionary urgency, and which sound out the missionary invitation. The message of Romans is not a treasure to be kept for the enjoyment of Christians. It is a trust to be shared with those who are not Christians. It declares to all men everywhere that "the wages of sin is death, but the free gift of God is eternal life through Jesus Christ our Lord."

---

[1] Robertson, *op. cit.*, p. 428